RAINBOW PRAYER

- A -
with Apostles, **Mary**, Martyrs,
Virgins, Pastors & Doctors,
& Saintly Women & Men

- B -
Midday Work Hours

- C -
In Health & In Healing

- D -
Psalms of Francis of Assisi

meditation rendering by
Stephen Joseph Wolf

www.idjc.org

> *When **the rainbow** is in the clouds,*
> *I see her*
> *and remember the eternal covenant*
> *between God and every living creature*
> *of every kind on the earth.*
> *– said God*
>
> Genesis 9:16

Rainbow Prayer
Copyright © 2023
Stephen Joseph Wolf
All rights reserved. No part of this book may be copied or reproduced in any form or by any means, except for the inclusion of brief quotations in a review or the songs understood by the publisher to be in the public domain, without written permission of the publisher.

If you need the masculine pronouns for God in traditional translations, you will not like this rendering.

For the holy name *YHVH* or Yahweh, the Hebrew word for "My Lord" (***Adonai***) is used, pronounced ***ah-duh-'nigh***. See page 166 for other choices made in this meditation rendering.

ISBN 978-1-937081-73-7

ISBN 978-1-937081-79-9   *Rainbow Psalms in 30 Days*
with Canticles & Sayings of Jesus, 381 pages

ISBN 978-1-937081-74-4   *Dawn & Dusk Rainbow Prayer*
includes the seasons of Advent, Christmas, Lent & Easter
as well as Ordinary Time, 775 pages

ISBN 978-1-937081-70-0   *Dawn & Dusk Rainbow for Ordinary Time*
includes only Ordinary Time, 523 pages

printed and distributed by Ingram Books
published by IDJC Press
www.idjc.org

RAINBOW PRAYER

- A -
APOSTLES, MARY & OTHER SAINTS

is drawn from the Commons of Mary and the Saints and has proven especially helpful for those trying to discern whether they are being called to pray the *Liturgy of the Hours*.

- B -
MIDDAY WORK HOURS

is inspired by the psalms and readings of the Midday Hours and reflection on years of working as a student, paper boy, janitor, launderer, clerk, landscaper, accountant, and parish priest.

- C -
IN HEALTH & IN HEALING

has roots in a summer chaplaincy internship at Emory Hospital (the '96 Olympics), often offering short readings from the Psalter, and watching faithful Methodists, Baptists, Jews and others taking in the sacred word with a reverence that resembles a Catholic receiving holy communion. These passages gave great consolation then, and I often called on them in pastoral care. On the occassional day of depression, this is my breviary.

- D -
PSALMS of FRANCIS of ASSISI

is the collection of fragments of psalms and other scripture compiled in a short collection for Franciscan mendicant beggars, a small prayerbook arranged for the seasons of Advent, Christmas, Lent (and Ordinary Time) and Easter.

APOSTLES, MARY & OTHER SAINTS

Which Day Do I Use?

Check the *Calendar of Saints*.
Is this a saint day?
  A. *Yes:*
    Use the set for this variety of saint.
  B. *No:*
    Use the set for the day of the week.

SEQUENCE

1. **Psalms and Canticles**
2. **Reading**
3. **Responsory**
4. **Gospel Canticle, or Gospel of the Day** *
5. **Intercessions**
6. **Closing Prayer**
7. **Lord's Prayer**

Keep it simple. Use what is helpful. Skip what is not. You may wish to spend some time in silence after each psalm, canticle or reading, even if for a couple of minutes. **But keep it simple**.

* Experiment with the Gospel Canticles (see pages 172-74) and with the Gospel reading of the day (pages 154-164) from your Bible, **but keep it simple**.

HOW TO USE THIS BOOK

I take off my shoes, sit up, offer up my still incomplete awareness of the illusions by which I live, and ask God to speak God's name in the center of my soul.

Then I make the Sign of the Cross with the opening prayer.

For each Psalm or Canticle, I recite the Antiphon, then the full poem, a trinitarian Doxology as provided, and then the Antiphon is repeated.

For the other parts, simply pray as indicated or as you wish. **But keep it simple**.   - Steve Wolf

RAINBOW PRAYER

APOSTLES, MARY & OTHER SAINTS

	UNAPPROVED CALENDAR of SAINTS & HOLYs	6
SUNDAY	APOSTLES (any time of day)	25
MONDAY	MARTYRS	30
TUESDAY	HOLY WOMEN	35
WEDNESDAY	PASTORS & DOCTO R S	41
THURSDAY	HOLY MEN	47
FRIDAY	VIRGINS	52
SATURDAY	MARY	57

	MIDDAY WORK HOURS		IN HEALTH & IN HEALING	
	Morning	Afternoon	Morning	Evening
SUNDAY	62	64	92	94
MONDAY	66	68	96	98
TUESDAY	70	72	100	102
WEDNESDAY	73	76	104	106
THURSDAY	78	81	108	110
FRIDAY	83	86	113	115
SATURDAY	88	90	117	120

PSALMS of FRANCIS of ASSISI

	SUN	MON	TUE	WED	THU	FRI	SAT
ADVENT	123	124	124	126	127	128	130
CHRISTMAS	131	131	133	131	135	131	133
LENT *(& Ord.)*	136	137	139	140	142	144	146
EASTER	148	150	151	148	150	151	152

DAILY GOSPEL READINGS	154 - 164
LECTIO DIVINA	165
CHOICES MADE & ACKNOWLEDGMENTS	166
INDEX of PSALMS, CANTICLES, & READINGS	170
CANTICLE of ZECHARIAH (in The Morning)	172
CANTICLE of MARY (in The Evening)	173
CANTICLE of SIMEON (at Night)	174
CLOSING PRAISES of FRANCIS of ASSISI	175

Calendar of Saints & Holys
solemnities, feasts, memorials, optional memorials,
plus civic holy days and lgbtq+ holys

JANUARY

1 **Solemnity: Mary, the Mother of God** Luke 2:16-21
   Robert Nugent, 2014, cofounder New Ways Ministry
   Emancipation Proclamation, 1863
2 Basil the Great, 379, & Gregory Nazianzen, 389, bishops & doctors
   Kwanzaa concludes
3 Holy Name of Jesus
   Humility Day
4 Elizabeth Ann Seton, 1821, widow&founder, Sisters of Charity
5 John Neumann, 1860, bishop of Philadelphia
   George Washington Carver, 1943, scientist
   Twelfth Night
6 Andre Bessette of Montreal, 1937, worker & religious
   World Day for Orphans
7 Raymond of Penyafort, OP, 1275, prest
   (Monday after January 6) Plough Monday
8 *Jeanne Manford, 2013, founder of PFLAG*
9 *International Choreographers Day*
10 *League of Nations Day*
   David Bowie, 2016, musician
11 *Human Trafficking Awareness Day*
12 Aelred of Rivaulx, 1167, Trappist abbot
   Earthquake in Haiti, 2010
13 Hilary of Poitiers, 368, bishop & doctor
   George Fox, 1699, Quakers founder
   (Third Monday in January) Martin Luther King, Jr. Day
17 Anthony of Egypt, 356, hermit & abbot
   Mary Oliver, 2019, poet
   1st execution after death penalty reinstated, 1977
18-25 Week of Prayer for Christian Unity

20 Sebastian of Rome, 288?, martyr
   Fabian, 250, pope & martyr
   ACLU founded, 1920
   Disc Jockey Day
21 Agnes, beg. of 4th C. @ age 12, virgin & martyr
   Thank Your Mentor Day
22 Day of prayer for legal protection of unborn children(USA)
   (Jan 23 if the 22nd is a Sunday)
23 Vincent of Valencia in Spain, early 4th C., deacon & martyr
   Marianne Cope of Moloka'i, 1918, Sister of St Francis
24 Francis de Sales, 1622, bishop of Geneva & doctor
   Thurgood Marshall, 1993, Supreme Court justice
   'Being homosexual is not a crime.' Pope Francis, 2023
25 **Feast: Conversion of Paul, Apostle**   Mark 16:15-18
   Jonathan Larson, 1996, composer & playwright
26 **Timothy & Titus, bishops**   Luke 10:1-9
   Birthday of Lotus 1-2-3, 1983
27 Angela Merici, 1540, virgin
   Holocaust Remembrance Day; Auschwitz-Birkenau liberated,1945
28 Thomas Aquinas, 1274, priest & doctor, Dominican
   Community Engagement Day
29 *Common Sense Day; Thomas Paine born, 1737*
30 *Martyrs Day; Mahatma Gandhi assassinated, 1948*
31 John Bosco, 1888, inspired founding, Salesians, priest & teacher

FEBRUARY

African-American History Month
1 *Freedom Day; Lincoln signs 13th amendment, 1863*
2 **Feast: Presentation of the Lord**   Luke 2:22-40
  Groundhog Day; Candlemas Day
  (*Sunday after February 2*) World Day for Consecrated Life
3 Blaise, early 4th C., bishop of Sebaste in Armenia & martyr
  (*Blessing of Throats* on this day or Sunday near Feb 3)
  Ansgar, 865, bishop, Benedictine
4 *Liberace, 1987, pianist*

February, continued

- 5 Agatha of Sicily, mid 3rd C., virgin & martyr
- 6 Paul Miki, SJ, and Companions, 1597, all martyrs, Nagasaki
- 7 *Send a Card to a Friend Day*
- 8 Jerome Emiliani, 1537, priest
  Josephine Bakhita, 1947, virgin
  World Day of Prayer and Awareness against Human Trafficking
- 10 Scholastica of Nursia, 543, virgin, Benedictine
- 11 Our Lady of Lourdes, apparition to St. Bernadette in 1858
  World Day of the Sick
  Nelson Mandela freed, 1990
  Satisfied Staying Single Day
- 12 *Abraham Lincoln born, 1809; NAACP founded 1909*
  Red Hand Day, the right of children to not be soldiers
- 14 Cyril, 869, and Methodius, 885, monks & bishops
  Valentine's Day
  Frederick Douglas, 1817, chosen birthday
  National Donor Day
- 15 *Parinirvana (Nirvana) Day, marks the death of Buddha, 183 BC*
  Singles Awareness Day
  (Third Monday in February) Presidents Day
  (Third Friday in February) National Caregivers Day
- 16 *Kyoto Protocol Day, to reduce greenhouse gas emissions, 2005*
- 17 Seven Founders of the Order of Servites, mid 13thC Florence
- 18 *Michelangelo Buonarotti, 1564, artist*
  Matthew Kelty, 2011, Trappist monk
- 19 *Japanese-American concentration camps established in US, 1942*
  Sylvia Rivera, 2002, trans stonewall activist
- 20 *World Day of Social Justice*
  Nat'l Day of Soidarity with Muslim, Arab, South Asian Immigrants
- 21 Peter Damian, 1072, bishop of Ostia & doctor
  Malcolm X, 1965, Muslim human rights activist
  Paul Farmer, 2022, physician & cofounder Partners In Health:
  "The idea that some lives matter less is the root of all that is wrong."
  Language Day

CALENDAR of SAINTS & HOLYs

22 **Feast: Chair of Peter, Apostle**　　　　Matthew 16:13-19
   Andy Warhol, 1987, artist
23 Polycarp, 155, bishop of Smyrna & martyr burned at stake
24 *Russia invaded Ukraine, 2022*
25 *Avertanus & Romeo, 1380, patrons of AIDS pandemic*
   Tennessee Williams, 1983, playwright
26 *Black Lives Matter Day; Trayvon Martin age 17 killed in 2012*
27 Gregory of Narek, 1011, monk & doctor
   Fred Rogers, 2003, Mr Rogers
   World NGO Day

MARCH

1 *Brady Gun Bill, 1994*
  Zero Discrimination Day
  International Women of Color Day
2 *Sioux Act, 1889, reduces Native American reservations to present size*
  Theodor Seuss Geisel (Dr. Seuss) born, 1904;
  (schoolday nearest Mar 2) Read Across America Day
3 Katherine Drexel, 1955, virgin & founder Missionary Sisters
  World Day of Prayer
4 Casimir of Poland, 1484, prince
7 Perpetua and Felicity of Carthage, 203, martyrs
  Harris Glenn Milstead (Divine), 1988, actor/singer/drag queen
8 John of God, 1550, founder in Spain of Order of Hospitallers
  (Second Sunday in March, 2 am) Daylight Savings Time ends
9 Frances of Rome, 1440, religious
10 *Harriet Tubman, 1913, abolitionist*
11 *Gandhi's Salt March begins, 1930*
   PFLAG founded, originally Parents & Friends of Lesbians & Gays, 1973
12 Symeon the New Theologian, 1022
   Aztec New Year
13 *Susan B. Anthony, 1906, abolitionist, suffragist*
   Good Samaritan Day
14 *Pi Day; Write Your Story Day*
15 *International Day to Combat Islamophobia*

March, continued

16 *Freedom of Information Day; James Madison born 1751*
17 Patrick of Ireland, 461, bishop of Armagh
18 Cyril of Jerusalem, 386, bishop of Jerusalem & doctor
   Forgive Mom & Dad Day (try praying Psalm 131)
19 **Solemnity: Joseph, Spouse of Mary**   Matthew 1:16-24a
20 *Won't You Be My Neighbor Day; Fred Rogers born 1928*
21 *International Day for the Elimination of Racial Discrimination*
   69 killed in Sharpeville, South Africa, 1960
   Selma March begins, 1965
23 Turibius of Mogrovejo, 1606, bishop
24 *Oscar Romero, 1980, martyr*
25 **Solemnity: The Annunciation of the Lord**   Luke 1:26-38
26 *Walt Whitman, 1892, poet*
27 *Patrick "Pax" Nidorf, OSA, 2023, founder Dignity USA*
   World Theatre Day
30 *Thea Bowman, FSPA, 1990, religious sister*
31 *Gilbert Baker, 2017, creator of the rainbow flag*
   Transgender Day of Visibility

APRIL

1 *April Fools Day*
2 Francis of Paola, 1507, hermit
4 Isidore, bishop of Seville & doctor
  Martin Luther King, Jr. killed, 1968
5 Vincent Ferrer, 1419, priest
  International Day of Conscience
6 *International Asexuality Day*
7 John Baptist de La Salle, 1719, founder of Christian Brothers
  Public Television Day
10 Teilhard de Chardin, SJ, 1955, priest & scientist
   Siblings Day
11 Stanislaus, 1079, bishop of Cracow & martyr
   Jackie Robinson's first major league baseball game, 1947
   Pacem in Terris by Pope John XXIII, 1963

CALENDAR of SAINTS & HOLYs

13 Martin I, 655, pope & martyr
17 *Student Nonviolent Coordinationg Committee (SNCC) formed, 1960*
14 *Rachel Carson, 1964, marine biologist*
   Pax Christi USA founded, 1972
   (Third Wednesday in April) Youth Homelessness Matters Day
18 *Albert Einstein, 1955, physicist*
20 *National High Five Day, invented by black gay Glenn Burke, 1977*
21 Anselm, 1109, bishop of Canterbury & doctor
22 *Earth Day*
   Day of Silence (LGBTQ youth and allies)
   Barry "Dame Edna" Humphries, 2023, drag comedian
23 George, about 303, martyr
   Adalbert, 997, bishop & martyr
   Cesar Chavez, 1993, farmworkers activist
24 Fidelis of Sigmaringen, 1622, priest & martyr
   Armenian Genocide Remembrance Day, 1914-18
25 **Feast: Mark, Evangelist**   Mark 16:15-20
   Blessing of Fields & Flocks
26 *Arbor Day*
   Lesbian Visibility Day
28 Louis Grignion de Montfort, 1716, priest
   Peter Chanel, 1841, priest & martyr
   First Rally for the Disappeared by Mothers in Argentina, 1977
   Stop Food Waste Day
29 Catherine of Siena, O.P. 3rd Order, 1380, virgin & doctor
   International Dance Day
30 Pius V, 1572, pope & religious
   Honesty Day; Bugs Bunny Day

MAY

1 **Joseph the Worker, carpenter**   Matthew 13:54-58
  Blessing of Tools & Equipmet for Work
  (First Thursday in May) National Day of Prayer
2 Athanasius, 373, bishop of Alexandria & doctor
  Leonardo da Vinci, 1519, artist

May, continued

3 **Feast: Philip and James, Apostles**   John 14:6-14
Christine Jorgensen, 1989, trans activist
National Public Radio Day

4 *International Firefighters Day*
May the Fourth Be With You

5 *Vesak, birth of Buddha, 490 BC*
Cinco de Mayo

6 *words monosexual, homosexual, & heterosexual*
first used by Karoly Kertbeny, 1868
First Nazi book burning, 1933, library of the Institute of Sexology
National Nurses Day; Nurses Week begins

8 Julian of Norwich, 1416, nun & poet
Red Cross & Red Crescent Day; Henry Dunant founder b. 1828
VE Day, end of World War II in Europe, 1945
(Second Sunday in May) Mothers' Day

10 John of Avila, 1569, priest & doctor
Damian de Veuster of Moloka'i, Hawaii, 1889, leper & priest

12 Nereus & Achilleus, end of 1st C, martyrs
Pancras, about 304, martyr
National Nurses Week ends; Florence Nightingale born, 1820

13 Our Lady of Fatima

14 **Feast: Matthias, Apostle**   John 15:9-17
Magnus Hirschfeld, 1935, founder of the Institute of Sexology

15 Isidore of Madrid, 1130, farmer
Blessing of Seeds
Peter Maurin, 1949, cofounder of Catholic Workers
Peace Officers Memorial Day
Conscientious Objectors Day
(Third Saturday in May) Armed Forces Day

16 *Honor our LGBT Elders Day*
Waiters Day

17 *Brown v. Board of Education, 1954*
International Day Against Homophobia, Transphobia & Biphobia;
Homosexuality no longer treated as a mental disorder(WHO) 1990

CALENDAR of SAINTS & HOLYs

18 John I, 526, pope & martyr
19 *Agender Pride Day*
20 Bernardine of Siena, 1440, Franciscan priest
21 Christopher Magallanes & 24 Companions, 1915-37, martyrs
22 Rita of Cascia, 1457, Augustinian religious
24 *World Day of Prayer for the Church in China*
   Pansexual & Panromantic Awareness Day
   Storme DeLarverie, 2014, drag king & stonewall activist
25 Venerable Bede, 735, Benedictine priest & doctor
   Gregory VII, 1085, pope & religious
   Mary Magdalene de'Pazzi, 1607, virgin
   African Liberation Day
   (Last Monday in May) Memorial Day
26 Philip Neri, 1595, priest & founder of the Oratorians
27 Augustine of Canterbury, 604, bishop
28 *Amnesty International Day*
29 Paul VI, 1978, pope
30 *Joan of Arc, 1431, teen warrior*
31 **Feast: Visitation of Mary and Elizabeth**　　　Luke 1:39-56
   Tulsa Massacre, 1921

JUNE

Pride Month
1 Justin of Samaria & Rome, 165, martyr
2 Marcellinus & Peter, about 303, martyrs
   Native Americans became United States citizens, 1924
3 Charles Lwanga of Uganda, 21Companions,1885-87,martyrs
   Tiananmen Square, 1989
5 Boniface, Germany, 754, Benedictine abbot, bishop & martyr
   HIV Long-Term Survivers Day
6 Norbert of Magdeburg, 1134, bishop & founder
   Robert F. Kennedy, 1968, politician
7 *Alan Turing, 1954, mathemetician*
8 *Mohammed, 632, prophet*
9 Ephraim of Syria, 373, deacon & doctor

June, continued

11 **Barnabas, apostle**   Matthew 10:7-13
12 *Medgar Evers, 1963, civil rights activist*
    Pulse Remembrance Day, 49 killed in Orlando in 2016
    World Day Against Child Labor
13 Anthony of Padua, OFM, 1231, priest & doctor
    Thurgood Marshall on the Supreme Court, 1967
14 *Flag Day*
15 *Magna Carta Day, 1215*
    Bostock v.Clayton County, 2020, Civil Rights Law applies to LGBT
    (Third Sunday in June) Fathers' Day
17 *Geneva Protocol on biological chemical warfare, 1925*
    World Day to Combat Desertification and Drought
    Pope Francis thanks New Ways Ministry 'for your...work,' 2021
18 *International Day for Countering Hate Speech*
19 Romuald, 1027, abbot & founder of the Camaldolese
    Juneteenth, 1865, slaves emancipated in Galveston, Texas
20 *UN World Refugee Day*
21 Aloysius Gonzaga, 1591, age 23, Jesuit scholastic
    Cheny, Schwerner & Goodman killed in Mississippi, 1964
    World Day of Music
22 John Fisher & Thomas More of England, 1535, martyrs
    Paulinus of Nola, 431, bishop
    Judy Garland, 1969, singer
23 *International Olympic Day*
24 **Solemnity: Birth of John the Baptist**   Vigil: Luke 1:5-17
                                                                   Day: Luke 1:57-66,80
    Upstairs Lounge Fire, 1973, New Orleans, 32 killed
    International Fairy Day
    Upcycling Day
25 *Jeanne Manford & Morty, 1972, mother & gay son, marched with the Christopher Street Liberation Day after he had been beaten.*
    The Day of the Seafarer
26 *Lawrence v. Texas, "sodomy" laws unconstitutional, 2003*
    Obergefell v. Hodges, prohibiting gay marriage unconstitutional, 2015

CALENDAR of SAINTS & HOLYs

International Day of Support of Victims of Torture
27 Cyril of Alexandria, 444, bishop & doctor
PTSD Awareness Day
HIV Testing Day
28 Irenaeus of Lyons, 202, bishop & martyr
Stonewall Riots, *1969, Stonewall Inn onChristopherStreet,NYC*
First Rainbow Flag (8 colors) used in San Francisco, 1978
29 **Solemnity: Peter & Paul, Apostles**   Vigil: John 21:15-19
Day: Matthew 16:13-19
Hanns Neumann, 1978, auther The Men With the Pink Triangle,
story of Josef Kohout, d. 3-15-1994, gay survivor of the Nazi camps
International Day of Fishers
30 First Martyrs of Rome, 64
Queer Youth of Faith Rally

JULY

1 Blessed Junipero Serra of California, 1784, Franciscan priest
Harriet Beecher Stowe, 1896, author
Postal Workers Day
2 *Civil Rights Act of 1964*
Elie Wiesel, 2016, writer
3 **Feast: Thomas, Apostle**   John 20:24-29
Children strike for an 11-hour workday & a 6 day workweek,
in Patterson NY, 1835
4 Independence Day (USA)
Declaration of Independence, 1776
5 Elizabeth of Portugal, 1336,3rdOrd'rFranciscan,queen&widow
Anthony Zaccaria, 1539, priest
6 Maria Goretti of Corinaldi, 1902, age 12, virgin & martyr
Marsha P. Johnson, 1992, drag queen & stonewall activist
7 *Global Forgiveness Day*
9 Augustine Zhao Rong, 1815, priest
& Companions, 1648-1930, all martyrs
11 Benedict of Nursia, 547, abbot & founder of the Benedictines
12 *National Simplicity Day; Henry Thoreau born 1817*

July, continued

- 13 Henry II, 1024, emperor & husband to St. Cunegund
  Frida Kahla, 1954, artist
- 14 Blessed Kateri Tekakwitha of the Mohawks, 1680, virgin
  Karl Heinrich Ulrichs, 1895, sexology pioneer
  International Non-Binary People's Day
  National Nude Day
- 15 Bonaventure, OFM, 1274, bishop of Albano & doctor
- 16 Our Lady of Mount Carmel, 12th C. hermits
  First atomic weapons test, 1945
  International Drag Day
- 17 *International Justice Day*
- 18 Camillus de Lellis, 1614, priest & founder Clerks Regular
  Caravaggio, 1610, artist
  African Americans become United States citizens, 1868
- 20 Apolinaris, 1ˢᵗ C., bishop & martyr
  Apollo 11 lands on the moon, 1969
- 21 Lawrence of Brindisi, 1619, priest & doctor
  National Day of the Cowboy
- 22 **Feast: Mary Magdalene, Disciple**   John 20:1-2,11-18
- 23 Bridget of Sweden, 1373, religious
- 24 Sharbel Makhluf, 1898, monk & priest, Lebanese Maronite
  Cousins Day
- 25 **Feast: James, Apostle**   Matthew 20:20-28
  Hire a Veteran Day
- 26 Joachim and Ann, parents of Mary, grandparents of Jesus
  Grandparents Day
  Americans with Disabilities Act signed, 1990
- 28 *World Nature Conservation Day*
- 29 **Martha, Mary & Lazarus, Disciples**   John 11:19-27
  William Wilberforce, 1833, abolitionist
  "If someone is gay and searches for the Lord and has good will, who am I to judge?" - Pope Francis, 2013
- 30 Peter Chrysologus, mid 5th C., bishop of Ravenna & doctor
  International Day of Friendship
- 31 Ignatius of Loyola, 1556, priest & founder, Society of Jesus

CALENDAR of SAINTS & HOLYs

AUGUST

1. Alphonsus Liguori, 1787, founder: Redemptorists, bishop & doctor
2. Eusebius of Vercelli, 371, bishop
   Peter Julian Eymard, 1868, priest
3. *Flannery O'Connor, 1964, writer*
   Fellowship of Reconciliation founded 1914, Cologne train station
4. John Mary Vianney of Ars, 1859, patron of parish priests
5. Dedication of the Basilica of Saint Mary Major
6. **Feast: Transfiguration of the Lord**
       A Matthew 17:1-9   **B** Mark 9:2-10   **C** Luke 9:28b-36
   Hiroshima, 1945
7. Sixtus II, 258, pope & Companions, martyrs
   Cajetan, 1547, priest
8. Dominic, 1221, priest & founder: Order of Preachers (Dominicans)
9. Teresa Benedicta (Edith Stein), 1942 at Auschwitz, Carmelite, virgin & martyr
   Franz Jägerstätter, 1943, conscientious objector & martyr
   International Day of the World's Indigenous Peoples
   Nagasaki, 1945
10. **Feast: Lawrence, 258, Deacon & Martyr**   John 12:24-26
11. Clare of Assisi, 1253, virgin & founder of Poor Clares
12. Jane Frances de Chantal, 1641, religious
13. Pontian, pope & Hippolytus, priest, 235, martyrs
    Lefthanders Day
14. Maximilian Kolbe, OFM Conv, 1941 at Auschwitz, priest & martyr
15. **Solemnity: Assumption of Mary**   Vigil: Luke 11:27-28
                                                     Day: Luke 1:39-56
    India achieves independence, 1947
    Blessing of Produce
16. Stephen of Hungary, 1038, king
17. *National Nonprofit Day*
20. Bernard, 1153, Cistercian abbot of Clairvaux & doctor
21. Pius X, 1914, pope
22. Queenship of Mary
    (Last Saturday in August) Make Music on the Porch Day

August, continued

- 23 Rose of Lima, Peru, 1617, age 31, OP 3rd Order & virgin
  Remembrance of Slave Trade & its Abolition; Haiti, 1791
- 24 **Feast: Bartholomew, Apostle** John 1:45-51
  Bayard Rustin, 1987, advisor to MLK Jr
  Elijah McClain, age 23, 2019, human
- 25 Louis IX of France, 1270. King
  Joseph Calasanz, 1648, priest
- 26 *Women's Equality Day; 19th Amendment ratified in TN, 1920*
- 27 Monica of Tagaste in Africa, 387 in Ostia, mother of Augustine
  W.E.B. DuBois, 1963, sociologist
  'I Have a Dream' Speech by Martin Luther King, Jr., 1963
- 28 Augustine, 430, bishop of Hippo in Africa & doctor
- 29 **Martyrdom of John the Baptist** Mark 6:17-29

SEPTEMEBER

- 1 World Day of Prayer for the Care of Creation
  (First Monday in September) Labor Day
- 2 *Victory in Japan Day, 1945*
- 3 Gregory the Great, 604, monk, pope & doctor
- 4 *Albert Schweitzer, 1965, Lutheran theologian, physician, humanitarian*
- 5 Teresa of Calcutta, 1997, religious founder Sisters of Charity
  International Day of Charity
- 7 *International Day of Clean Air*
- 8 **Feast: Nativity of Mary** Matthew 1:1-16,18-23
  International Literacy Day
- 9 Peter Claver, SJ, 1654, priest & missionary to Columbia
- 10 *Suicide Prevention Day*
- 11 Mychal Judge, OFM, *2,763 souls at World Trade Center*, 2001
  Patriots Day
- 12 Most Holy Name of Mary
  Stephen Biko, 1977, anti-apartheid activist
- 13 John Chrysostom, 407, bishop of Constantinople & doctor
  Israel-PLO peace accord, 1993

CALENDAR of SAINTS & HOLYs

14 **Feast: The Exaltation of the Holy Cross** John 3:13-17
15 Our Lady of Sorrows Luke 2:33-35
   4 children killed by KKK in church bombing in Birmingham, 1963
   International Day of Democracy
16 Cornelius, 253, pope & martyr
   Cyprian, 258, bishop of Carthage & martyr
   Ozone Treaty, 1987
   Dance Day
17 Hildegard of Bingen, 1179, virgin & doctor
   Robert Bellarmine, 1621, Jesuit, bishop & doctor
   Constitution Day, ratified 1787
   Camp David Accords between Israel & Egypt, 1978
18 *Dag Hammarskjöld, 1961, diplomat*
19 Januarius, 305, bishop & martyr
20 Andrew Kim Taegon, 1847, priest, Paul Chong Hasang,
   catechist, & 101 Companions, martyrs in Korea
21 **Feast: Matthew, Apostle & Evangelist** Matthew 9:9-13
22 *Peace Corps founded, 1961*
   James Allison, 'The Fulcrum of Discovery,' 2009
   (being gay: a regularly occurring non-pathological
    minority variant in the human condition)
23 Pius (Padre Pio) of Pietrelcina, 1968, Capuchin priest
   Celebrate Bisexuality Day
26 Cosmas & Damian, 303, physicians & martyrs
27 Vincent de Paul, 1660, priest & founder: Vincentians & Daughters of Charity
   Ancestor Appreciation Day
28 Wenceslaus of Bohemia, 929, martyr
   Lawrence Ruiz & Companions, 1633-1637, Nagasaki, martyrs
29 **Feast: Michael, Gabriel, and Raphael,** Archangels John 1:47-51
   W.H. Auden, 1973, poet
   Confucius Day
30 Jerome of Bethlehem, 420, priest & doctor
   Rumi, Sufi poet, born 1207
   Translation Day

OCTOBER

LGBTQ History Month

1. Therese of the Child Jesus, 1897, Carmelite of Lisieux, virgin & doctor
   Always Our Children, US Bishops document, 1997
   International Music Day
   (First Monday in October) World Habitat Day
2. Guardian Angels   Matthew 18:1-5,10
   International Day of Non-Violence; Gandhi born 1869
   Rock Hudson, 1985, actor
4. Francis of Assisi, 1221, founder, Order of the Franciscans
5. Faustina Kowalska, 1938, virgin
   Bl Francis Xavier Seelos, 1867, priest, Redemptorist
6. Bruno, 1101, priest
   Bl Marie-Rose Durocher, 1849, virgin & founder, Sisters of the Holy Name
   Metropolitan Community Church founded, Huntington Park CA, 1968
   Matthew Shepard, age 21, 1998, human
   World Cerebral Palsy Day
7. Our Lady of the Rosary
   Sergius & Bachus, 3rd C., soldiers & martyrs
8. *International Lesbian Day*
   (Second Monday in October) Columbus Day, 12 October, 1492
   (Second Monday in October) Indigenous Peoples' Day
9. Denis, bishop of Paris, & 2 Companions, mid 3rd C., martyrs
   John Leonardi, 1609, priest
   John Henry Newman, converted 1845, cardinal
11. John XXIII, pope, anniversary of 1962 opening of Vatican II
    Frank Kameny, 2011, founder Mattachine Society of Washington
    March on Washington for Lesbian & Gay Rights, 1988;
    Coming Out Day
14. Callistus I, 222, pope & martyr
15. Teresa of Avila, 1582, Carmelite, virgin & doctor
    (Third Wednesday in October) International Pronoun Day
    (Third Thursday in October) Spirit Day: Wear Purple
16. Margaret Mary Alacoque, 1690, Sister of the Visitation & virgin
    Hedwig, 1243, religious

CALENDAR of SAINTS & HOLYs

- 17 Ignatius of Antioch, 107, bishop & martyr in Rome
- 18 **Feast: Luke, Evangelist** — Luke 10:1-9
- 19 Isaac Jogues, SJ, John de Brebeuf, SJ, &Companions,1640's,martyrs
- 20 Paul of the Cross, 1775, priest & founder of the Passionists
- 22 John Paul II, pope, anniversary of 1978 inauguration
- 23 John of Capistrano, 1456, priest, Franciscan
- 24 Anthony Mary Claret, 1870, bishop
  United Nations Day
- 25 *Fine Art Appreciation Day*
- 26 *Elizabeth Cady Stanton, 1902, womens vote activist*
  Intersex Awareness Day; 1st protest to American Academy of Pediatrics, 1996
- 28 **Feast: Simon and Jude, Apostles** — Luke 6:12-16
  National Immigrants Day
- 31 *All Hallowed Eve*

NOVEMBER

- 1 **Solemnity: All Saints** — Matthew 5:1-12a
  (First Sunday in November, 2 am) Daylight Savings Time ends
- 2 **All Souls**   Matt 5:1-12a   Matt 11:25-30   Matthew 25:31-46
  Luke 7:11-17   Lk 23:44-24:6a   Lk 24:13-16,28-35
  John 5:24-29   John 6:37-40   John 6:51-58
  John 11:17-27   John 11:32-45   John 14:1-6
- 3 Martin de Porres of Lima in Peru, OP, 1639, religious
- 4 Charles Borromeo, 1584, bishop of Milan
- 7 *Touko Laaksonen, 1991, artist*
- 8 *Intersex Solidarity Day; Herculine Barbin, born 1838*
- 9 **Feast: Dedication of John Lateran Basilica** — John 2:13-22
  Kristallnacht, 1938
  Berlin Wall came down, 1989
- 10 Leo the Great, 461, pope & doctor
- 11 Martin of Tours, 397, bishop & founder of 1st monastery in the West
  Veterans Day (if a Sunday, then the 12th), Armistice Day, 11 pm, 1918
- 12 Josaphat, 1623, monk, bishop of Polotsk & martyr
- 13 Frances Xavier Cabrini, 1917, virgin & founder Sisters of the Sacred Heart
- 14 *Booker T. Washington, 1915, civil rights activist*

November, continued

- 15 Albert the Great, OP, 1280, bishop of Ratisbon & doctor
  Margaret Mead, 1978, anthropologist
- 16 Margaret of Scotland, 1093, spouse & mother
  Gertrude of Saxony, 1301, virgin, Benedictine
  Will D. Campbell, 2009, Baptist preacher & civil rights activist
  International Day of Tolerance
- 17 Elizabeth of Hungary,1231, queen & 3rd Order Franciscan
  Audre Lorde, 1992, poet
- 18 Rose Philippine Duchesne, 1852 in St. Louis MO, virgin
  Dedication of the Basilicas of Saints Peter & Paul
- 19 *Gettysburg Address of Abraham Lincoln, 1863*
  Club Q, 2022, 5 killed, Colorado Springs, CO
- 20 *Nuremburg War Trials begin, 1945*
  Transgender Day of Remembrance
- 21 Presentation of Mary
- 22 Cecilia, 3rd century?, virgin & martyr
  John F. Kennedy, 1963, politician
  (4th Thursday) Thanksgiving Day (USA) Lk 10:21-24 or Lk 17:11-19
- 23 Columban, 615, abbot
  Clement I, about 100, pope & martyr
  Miguel Agustin Pro, SJ, 1927, priest & martyr in Mexico
  Day of Charity, Penance & Prayer for Economic Justice
- 24 Andrew Dung-Lac, 1839, priest
  & 116 Companions, martyrs in Vietnam
  Freddie Mercury, 1991, singer & composer
- 26 *Sojourner Truth, 1883, abolitionist*
- 27 *Harvey Milk, 1978, gay politician killed*
  (Tuesday after Thanksgiving Day) Giving Tuesday
- 29 *Dorothy Day, 1980, cofounder Catholic Worker*
- 30 **Feast: Andrew, Apostle**   Matthew 4:18-22
  Oscar Wilde, 1900, poet & playwright
  Mother Jones, 1930, labor organizer
  Etty Hillesum, 1943, diarist
  (Sunday nearest to November 30) First Sunday of Advent

CALENDAR of SAINTS & HOLYs

DECEMBER

1. *James Baldwin, 1987, writer & civil rights activist*
   Rosa Parks Day, arrested for keeping her seat on that bus, 1955
   World AIDS Day
3. Francis Xavier, SJ, 1552, priest & missionary
4. John of Damascus, 749, priest & doctor
5. *Prohibition repealed, 1933*
6. Nicholas, 350, bishop of Myra (now in Turkey)
7. Ambrose, 397, bishop of Milan & doctor
8. **Solemnity: Immaculate Conception of Mary**   Luke 1:26-47
   Pansexual Pride Day
9. Juan Diego of Tepayac, Mexico, 1531, apparition Our Lady of Guadalupe
   Genocide Prevention Day
10. Our Lady of Loreto
    United Nations Declaration of Human Rights, 1948
    Thomas Merten, 1968, Trappist monk & writer
    Adele Starr, 2010, first president of PFLAG
11. Damasus I, 384, pope
    UNICEF created, 1946
12. **Feast: Our Lady of Guadalupe**   Luke 1:26-38 *or* 39-47
    Universal Health Coverage Day
13. Lucy of Syracuse, 304, virgin & martyr
14. John of the Cross, 1591, founder Discalced Carmelites, priest & doctor
    Sandy Hook Elementary shooting, 2012, 20 children & 6 adults killed
    COVID vaccinations begin, 2020
15. *Bill of Rights ratified, 1791*
17. Advent 'O' Antiphons begin
18. *International Migrants Day*
21. Peter Canisius, SJ, 1597, missionary, priest & doctor
23. John of Kanty, 1473, priest
    Festivus

RAINBOW PRAYER
December, continued

25 **Solemnity: Nativity of the Lord, Christmas**   see page 154
26 **Feast: Stephen, Deacon & First Martyr**   Matthew 10:17-22
   Kwanzaa begins
27 **Feast: John, Apostle & Evangelist**   John 20:1a,2-8
28 **Feast: The Holy Innocents, Martyrs**   Matthew 2:13-18
   Endangered Species Act, 1973
   Call a Friend Day
29 Thomas Becket, 1170, bishop of Canterbury & martyr
   David & Jonathan, intimate friends
   Wounded Knee Massacre, 1890
31 Sylvester I, 335, pope
   New Year's Eve

APOSTLES SUNDAY

+ Lord, give me wisdom to seek your face.
Open the eyes and ears of my heart
and help me to see and hear as you desire.

PSALM 117

Antiphon   *Calling many to follow him,*
Jesus chose twelve and made them apostles.

Praise Adonai, all you nations;
and give glory, all you peoples.

Great is this steadfast love toward us;
the fidelity of Adonai to forever.

Hallelujah!

Glory to the Father and to the Son and to the Holy Spirit,
As it was in the beginning, is now, and will be forever; Amen.

Repeat antiphon.

PSALM 126

Antiphon *I came and went among you*
as a servant to all.

When Adonai restored Zion out of captivity
we felt like people in a dream.
Then our mouth was filled with laughter,
and our tongue with a song of joy.

Then they said among the nations
"Their Adonai did great things for them."
Adonai did great things for us;
we were full of joy.

Restore our good fortune, Adonai,
like streams in the Negev desert.
Sowers are now in tears;
they will reap with a song of joy.

Going out, the sower goes out weeping,
carrying seeds for the sowing.
Returning, the sower will return
carrying sheaves with a song of joy.

Glory to the Father and to the Son and to the Holy Spirit,
As it was in the beginning, is now, and will be forever; Amen.

Antiphon

EPHESIANS 1:3-10

Antiphon   *I now call you my friends;*
hear what I have heard from my Abba.

Blessed be the God and Abba
of our Lord Jesus Christ,
who has blessed us in Christ
with every spiritual blessing in the heavens.

God chose us in Christ
before the foundation of the world,
to be holy and free of blemish before him.

In love, God gave us a destiny:
as parents adopt, through Jesus Christ himself,
in accord with the good pleasure of God's will
to the praise of the glory of grace
by which we are favored as God's beloved.

In Christ we have the redemption,
through his blood the forgiveness of sins
in accord with the riches of his grace
which he made abound to us.

In all wisdom and intelligence
the mystery of God's will is made known to us
in accord with God's good pleasure and purpose:

Ephesians 1:3-10, continued

> A stewardship of the fullness of time,
> heading up all things in Christ,
> the things in the heavens and the things on earth.

Glory to the Father and to the Son and to the Holy Spirit,
As it was in the beginning, is now, and will be forever; Amen.

Antiphon *I now call you my friends;*
hear what I have heard from my Abba.

READING **EPHESIANS 2:11-22**

And so you are no longer strangers and aliens, but you are equal citizens with the saints and members of the family of God, having been built on the foundation of the apostles and prophets, with the very self of Christ Jesus as the cornerstone, in whom the whole building fits together and grows into a holy temple in the Lord, in whom you also are being built together into a dwelling place of God in the spirit.

RESPONSORY Let the world see and know
that we live by your teachings.

GOSPEL ANTIPHON

You did not choose me, but I chose you
to be my witnesses to all the earth.

APOSTLES - SUNDAY

INTERCESSIONS   for the people of God; the cosmos; the poor…

CLOSING PRAYER

> Almighty Abba,
> the apostles learned the way at the feet of your Son
> and were witnesses to his resurrection.
> Keep me close to you, Lord, and teach me
> what the apostles learned from your Son.
> Amen.

OUR ABBA

Our Father *or*	**Our Abba** in heaven,
who art in heaven,	your name
hallowed be thy name.	be honored
Thy kingdom come,	and your reign come
thy will be done	on earth as in heaven.
on earth as it is in heaven.	Give us
Give us this day	bread for the day,
our daily bread	forgive us our sins
and forgive us our trespasses	as we forgive others,
as we forgive those	and help us
who trespass against us,	resist temptation
and lead us	to do the bad
not into temptation	with grace
but deliver us from evil.	to do the good.
Amen.	Amen.

MARTYRS MONDAY

+ Lord, give me courage
   to say yes to my vocation.
   Free me from all fear
   except reverence for you.

PSALM 118

Antiphon   *Whoever declares their very self for me,*
I will declare my very self for them.

Give thanks to Adonai who is good,
whose love is to forever.

Let Israel now declare:
the love of the Lord to forever.
Let the house of Aaron declare:
the love of the Lord to forever.
Let those who fear Adonai declare:
the love of the Lord to forever.

In anguish I cried to Adonai
who answered me with freedom.
Adonai is with me, I will not be afraid. - -

What can any human do to me?
Before enmity I keep this in mind:
Adonai is with me, ready to help me.

Better to take refuge in Adonai
than to trust in the human;
Better to take refuge in Adonai
than to trust in a prince.

All of the nations surrounded me,
indeed did they surround me;
in the name of Adonai indeed I cut them.
They swarmed around me like bees,
they crackled like thorns in a fire;
in the name of Adonai indeed I cut them.

To push back they pushed me back to fall
but Adonai came to my help.
Adonai became my strength and my song
and became to me salvation.
Shout joy and victory in your tents, you just.

Adonai's right hand does a mighty thing,
Adonai's right hand lifted high.
Adonai's right hand does a mighty thing.
I will not die; I will live
and proclaim these deeds indeed.
To chasten, Adonai let me be chastened,
but did not give me to death.

Psalm 118, continued

Open for me the gates of the just;
I will enter through them
and give thanks to Adonai.
This is Adonai's gate,
where just ones may enter.
I will give thanks to you for you answered me
and you became to me salvation.

The stone the builders rejected
became the cornerstone.
With Adonai this happened
and it is marvelous in our eyes.
This is the day Adonai has made;
let us rejoice and be glad in it.

Adonai, save us now!
Adonai, grant success now!
Blessed is the one coming in the name of Adonai;
We bless you from the house of Adonai.
Our El Adonai has shined light onto us.

Join with leaf branches in the festal procession
up to the horns of the altar.
To you, my God, I will give thanks.
You, my God, I will give glory.
Give thanks to Adonai who is good,
whose love is to forever.

Glory to the *Ruler* and to the *Prophet* and to the *Holy Ruah,*
As it was in the beginning, is now, and will be forever; Amen.

MARTYRS - MONDAY

Antiphon *Whoever declares their very self for me,
I will declare my very self for them.*

REVELATION 4:11; 5:9,10,12

Antiphon *The one who loses their life in me
will find it today and to eternity.*

Worthy are you, our Lord and our God,
to receive the glory and honor and power,
for you have created all things,
and by your will all things were created and are.

Worthy are you to receive the scroll and unseal it
for you were sacrificed, and by your blood
ransomed for God those from every
tribe and tongue and people and nation.

You made of them for our God
a realm of royals and priests,
and thus will they reign over the earth.

Worthy is the Lamb, sacrificed to receive
the power and riches and wisdom and strength
and honor and glory and blessing.

Glory to the *Ruler* and to the *Prophet* and to the *Holy Ruah*,
As it was in the beginning, is now, and will be forever; Amen.

Antiphon

'Ruah' is the mighty wind in the Old Testament.

READING **ROMANS 8:35,37-39**

Who will separate us from the love of Christ? Affliction? Distress? Persecution? Famine? Nakedness? Peril? The Sword? But in all these things we overconquer through the one who has loved us.

For I am persuaded that not death, nor life, nor angels, nor rulers, nor present things, nor things coming, nor powers, nor height, nor depth, nor any other creature will be able to separate us from the love of God in Christ Jesus, our Lord.

RESPONSORY Those who are just in God's eyes
live with God as friends to forever.

GOSPEL ANTIPHON

*Blessed are they who suffer persecution
for the sake of justice;
the reign of heaven is theirs.*

INTERCESSIONS for the people of God; the cosmos; the poor...

CLOSING PRAYER

Almighty God,
only you can turn our weakness into strength.
You gave the martyrs the courage
to suffer death for Christ; give me the courage
to give faithful witness to you this day. Amen.

OUR ABBA...

HOLY WOMEN TUESDAY

+ Lord, give me right judgment
to discern your call in freedom.
Make me wise in the ways
you wish me to be wise.

PSALM 122

Antiphon *Lord, your servant rejoices
in your saving presence.*

I rejoiced with those saying to me,
"Let us go to the house of Adonai."
Our feet stand in your gates, Jerusalem.

Jerusalem is built like a city
formed together, a compact.
There the tribes go up, the tribes of Adonai.

Make it in Israel a statute
to praise the name of Adonai,
for there stand the thrones of justice,
the thrones of the house of David.

Psalm 122, continued

Pray for the peace of Jerusalem!
May those who love you be secure.
May peace be within your walls,
security within your citadels.

For the sake of my sisters and brothers and friends
I will say, "Now, peace be within you."
For the sake of the house of our God Adonai
I will seek your prosperity.

Glory to the *Rock* and to the *Physician* and to the *Consoler*,
As it was in the beginning, is now, and will be forever; Amen.

Antiphon *Lord, your servant rejoices
in your saving presence.*

PSALM 42

Antiphon *My soul is clinging to you, Lord,
at your right hand.*

As a deer breathes heavy for streams of water,
so my soul throbs for you, God.

My soul she thirsts for God, the living God.
When can I go and meet the faces of God?

My tears were food for me by day and by night,
while all day they said to me,
"Where is your God?"

These things I remember
as my soul pours out before me:
how I would go with the multitude
to lead them to the house of God
sounding shouts of joy and thanksgiving,
a festive throng!

Why are you downcast, my soul?
Why are you disturbed within me?
Put hope in God, whom I will yet praise,
the saving help and presence.

My God, within me my soul she is downcast.
For this I will remember you
from the land of Jordan and heights of Hermon,
from the Mount of Mizar:

Deep calls to deep in the roar of your waterfalls.
All your waves and breakers are swept over me.

By day Adonai directs love
and at night the song within me
is a prayer to the God of my life.

I say to El my Rock, "why do you forget me?
Why must I go about mourning,
oppressed by enmity?"

With mortal agony in my bones,
taunted by adversity,
while all day they say to me,
"Where is your God?"

Psalm 42, continued

Why are you downcast, my soul?
Why are you disturbed within me?
Put hope in God, whom I will yet praise,
my saving help and God.

Glory to the *Rock* and to the *Physician* and to the *Consoler*,
As it was in the beginning, is now, and will be forever; Amen.

Antiphon *My soul is clinging to you, Lord,
at your right hand.*

WISDOM 9:1-6,9-11

Antiphon *The clouds have rained down the just one
and earth has brought forth a savior.*

God of my ancestors, Lord of mercy,
who made all things by your word
and through your wisdom framed humanity
to be master of the creatures you have created,
and to govern the world in holiness and justice
and judge justly and with an upright heart,

give me Wisdom, your companion at your throne,
and do not reject me from among your children,
for I am your servant, born of your handmaid,
a feeble human with a short life
and a weak understanding of justice and laws.

Though a human be
ever so perfect in human eyes,
without your Wisdom that same one
will be of no account…

With you is Wisdom,* who knows your works
and was present when you created the world,
who knows what is pleasing in your eyes
and what is right in accord with your ordinances.

Send her forth from the holy heavens
and dispatch her from your majestic throne,
that she may labor beside me
and I may learn what pleases you.

For she knows and understands all things
and will guide me to prudence in my actions
and guard me in her magnificence.

Glory to the *Rock* and to the *Physician* and to the *Consoler*,
As it was in the beginning, is now, and will be forever; Amen.

Antiphon

---

*Sophia,
  Lady Wisdom

READING **ROMANS 12:1-2**

I appeal to you, brothers and sisters, through the compassion of God, to present your bodies as a living sacrifice, holy and well-pleasing to God, your worship and reasonable service. Be not conformed to this age, but be transformed by the renewal of your mind, that what you do may prove to be the will of God, the good and well-pleasing and perfect.

RESPONSORY   In loving presence
the Lord will help her and be with her.

GOSPEL ANTIPHON

> *The reign of heaven*
> *is like a merchant seeking fine pearls*
> *who finding one of great value*
> *gives every other treasure to possess it.*

INTERCESSIONS   for the people of God; the cosmos; the poor...

CLOSING PRAYER

Lord, shower us
with your wisdom and loving kindness.
By serving you as have your holy women,
may our faith and actions be pleasing to you.
Amen.

OUR ABBA...

PASTORS & DOCTORS WEDNESDAY

+ Lord, give me knowledge
  of what Jesus teaches
  known in the triumph of your mercy
  over judgment, even justice.

PSALM 148

Antiphon *You are the light of the world;*
a city set on a hill cannot be hidden.

Hallelujah!

Give praise from the heavens!
Give praise in the heights.
Give praise all you angels.
Give praise all you hosts.

Give praise sun and moon.
Give praise all stars shining.
Give praise, you heavens of the heavens
and waters above the heavens.

Psalm 148, continued

Let them praise the name Adonai,
who commanded and they were created,
who set them in place forever,
to forever the decree Adonai gave,
not to pass away.

Praise Adonai, you earth,
you sea creatures and all in the deep,
lightning and hail, snow and cloud,
wind of the storm, all who do Adonai's bidding,

you mountains and hills,
fruit trees and cedars,
wild animals and all cattle,
small creatures and birds of flight,

you rulers of the earth and the nations,
royals and all people ruling on earth,
young men and young women,
old folks and children:

Let them praise the name Adonai
whose name alone is exalted,
whose splendor is above earth and the heavens,

who raised a horn for the people,
praise of all the saints,
of the sons and daughters of Israel,
of people close to the Lord.

Hallelujah!

Glory to the *All Knowing* and to the *Teacher* and to the *Guide,*
As it was in the beginning, is now, and will be forever; Amen.

Antiphon *You are the light of the world;*
a city set on a hill cannot be hidden.

PSALM 113

Antiphon *God's gift of grace to my life*
is service to the gospel.

Hallelujah!

Praise, you who serve Adonai!
Praise the name Adonai!

Blessed be the name of Adonai
from now and to forevermore.
From the rising of the sun to its setting
praised be the name of Adonai.

Exalted over all the nations is Adonai,
the glory above the heavens.
Who is like our God Adonai,
sitting enthroned on high,
stooping to look down
on the heavens and the earth?

Psalm 148, continued

Adonai raises the poor from dust
and lifts up the needy from ash heaps
to sit with royals, the royals of the people,
and settles the childless woman in a home,
a happy mother of children.

Hallelujah!

Glory to the *All Knowing* and to the *Teacher* and to the *Guide*,
As it was in the beginning, is now, and will be forever; Amen.

Antiphon *God's gift of grace to my life*
      is service to the gospel.

PSALM 146

Antiphon *Let us search for the lost and*
      lead back those who have strayed.

Hallelujah!

Praise Adonai, my soul!
I will praise Adonai during my life;
I will sing praise to my God while I still am.

Trust neither royalty nor human beings
in whom there is no salvation.
Their spirit-breath departs,
and they return to the ground.
On that day their plans come to nothing.

Blessed are they whose help is the God of Jacob,
whose hope and God are Adonai,
the maker of heaven and earth
and the sea and all that is in them.

The one staying faithful to forever
defends justice for the oppressed
and gives food to the hungry.

Adonai sets prisoners free;
Adonai gives sight to the blind;
Adonai lifts those who are bowed down;
Adonai loves the just.

Adonai watches over alien strangers,
and sustains the orphan and the widow,
but frustrates the ways that are bad.
Adonai reigns to forever,
your God, Zion,
from generation to generation.

Hallelujah!

Glory to the *All Knowing* and to the *Teacher* and to the *Guide*,
As it was in the beginning, is now, and will be forever; Amen.

Antiphon

READING **WISDOM 7:13-14**

What I have learned about wisdom, this I freely share, without hiding her riches. For to mortal beings she is an inexhaustible treasure. Those who gain this treasure win friendship with God, who commends the wise with gifts that come from discipline.

RESPONSORY May all the peoples praise God
for God's wise ways in the saints.

GOSPEL ANTIPHON

*The one who not only teaches
but does what is right
will be counted great
in the reign of God.*

INTERCESSIONS for the people of God; the cosmos; the poor…

CLOSING PRAYER

Lord, you gave light to our ancestors
by the gospel preaching of pastors and doctors.
Help us to grow in the love and knowledge
of your Son, our Lord Jesus Christ.
Amen.

OUR ABBA…

HOLY MEN THURSDAY

+ Lord, give me reverence
for the ways of our Abba
through the holiness
that comes only from you.

PSALM 93

Antiphon   *Lord, reveal the hidden things;*
show yourself to all people.

Adonai reigns, robed in majesty;
robed is Adonai and armed with strength.

The world is firmly established;
she cannot be moved.
Your throne was set up from long ago;
from eternity you are.

The seas lifted up, Adonai,
the seas lifted up their voice;
the seas lifted up their pounding.

Psalm 93, continued

More than thunders of great waters
or mighty breakers of the sea,
mighty in the height is Adonai.

Your statutes stand very firm;
your house, Adonai, is adorned in holiness
for length of days.

Glory to the *Almighty* and to the *Savior* and to the *Advocate*,
As it was in the beginning, is now, and will be forever; Amen.

Antiphon *Lord, reveal the hidden things;*
show yourself to all people.

DANIEL 3:57-90

Antiphon *Let all the earth bless the Lord.*

Bless the Lord, all you works of the Lord,
exalt and sing praise to forever.
Angels of the Lord, bless the Lord,
You heavens, bless the Lord,
All you waters above the heavens, bless the Lord,
All you powers, bless the Lord,
Sun and moon, bless the Lord,
Stars of heaven, bless the Lord.

HOLY MEN - THURSDAY

All you rain and dew, bless the Lord,
All you winds, bless the Lord,
You fire and heat, bless the Lord,
You ice and cold, bless the Lord,
You dews and falling snows, bless the Lord,
You snows and frosts, bless the Lord,
You nights and days, bless the Lord,
You light and darkness, bless the Lord,
You lightning and clouds, bless the Lord.

Let the earth bless the Lord,
exalt and sing praise to forever.
You mountains and hills, bless the Lord,
All things growing in the ground, bless the Lord,
You seas and rivers, bless the Lord,
You springs and rain, bless the Lord,
You sea monsters and swimmers, bless the Lord,
All you birds of the air, bless the Lord,
All you wild beasts and cattle, bless the Lord,
You sons and daughters, bless the Lord.

O Israel, bless the Lord,
exalt and sing praise to forever.
You priests of the Lord, bless the Lord,
You servants of the Lord, bless the Lord,
You spirits and souls of the just, bless the Lord,
You holy and humble in heart, bless the Lord,
Hananiah, Azariah, and Mishael, bless the Lord,
exalt and sing praise to forever...

Daniel 3:57-90, continued

Give thanks to the Lord, who is good,
whose mercy endures to forever.
Bless the God of "gods"
all you who worship the Lord;
sing praise and give thanks to the One God
whose mercy endures to forever.

(*No doxology*)

Antiphon   *Let all the earth bless the Lord.*

REVELATION 15:3b-4

Antiphon   *The earth will sing the melody of heaven,*
the saints singing before the throne.

Great and wonderful are your works,
Lord God Almighty.
Just and true are your ways,
Ruler of the nations.

Who will not fear, O Lord,
or glorify your name?

Only you are holy.
All the nations will come
and worship before you;
your ordinances are shown to all.

Glory to the *Almighty* and to the *Savior* and to the *Advocate*,
As it was in the beginning, is now, and will be forever; Amen.

Antiphon

HOLY MEN - THURSDAY

READING   **PHILIPPIANS 3:7-9a**

The things that were gain to me, these I now deem as loss on account of Christ. I deem all things to be loss measured against the excellence of knowing Christ Jesus my Lord, on account of whom I suffered all things as loss and deem them rubbish, so that I might gain Christ and be found in him.

RESPONSORY   The Lord wraps them in a splendid robe
of love and the glory of God.

GOSPEL ANTIPHON

> *The eyes of the Lord*
> *are on those who fear the Lord,*
> *on those who hope in God's mercy.*

INTERCESSIONS   for the people of God; the cosmos; the poor...

CLOSING PRAYER

Loving God,
you are the One who is holy;
without you nothing is good.
Help us to become
the holy people you call us to be.
Amen.

OUR ABBA...

VIRGINS FRIDAY

+ Lord, give me understanding
of our baptism in Christ
and set fire in me your confirming love.

PSALM 63:1-8

Antiphon *I worship with my whole being;*
my longing for Christ is to forever.

God, you are my God; you I earnestly seek.
My soul, she thirsts for you,
my body, he longs for you,
as in a land with no water, dry and weary.

So in the sanctuary I saw you,
beheld you in your power and glory.
Your love is better than life itself;
my lips will glorify you.

So I will praise you in all the ways I am alive;
calling your name I will lift up my hands.
As with fatness and richness,
my soul will be satisfied;
with singing lips my mouth will sing praise.

When I remember you on my bed,
through night watches I think of you,
you who are my help;
then in the shadow of your wings I sing.
My very self stays close to you;
your right hand upholds me.

Glory to the *Friend* and to the *Brother* and to the *Holy Sister*,
As it was in the beginning, is now, and will be forever; Amen.

Antiphon

PSALM 147:12-20

Antiphon *Lord, we follow you in hope and awe;*
we long to see your face.

Glorify Adonai, Jerusalem!
Zion, now give praise!

Your God strengthens the bars of your gates,
blesses your peoples within you,
brings peace to your border,
and satisfies you with finest of wheat.

Psalm 147:12-20, continued

Your God sends a command to the earth,
and swiftly runs a word,
spreading snow like the wool
and scattering frost like the ash.

Hail is hurled like pebbles;
who can stand before the icy blast?
The word of the Lord is sent, and they melt;
wind stirs up and the waters flow.

The word of the Lord is revealed to Jacob,
decrees and laws of the Lord to Israel.
Not for another nation did the Lord do this;
they do not know these laws.
Hallelujah!

Glory to the *Friend* and to the *Brother* and to the *Holy Sister*,
As it was in the beginning, is now, and will be forever; Amen.

Antiphon *Lord, we follow you in hope and awe;*
we long to see your face.

PSALM 127

Antiphon *Blessed are the pure of heart,*
for they shall see God.

If Adonai does not build the house,
the builders labor in vanity.
If Adonai does not watch over the city,
the watcher stands guard in vain.

VIRGINS - FRIDAY

It is vanity to rise early or stay up late,
or to eat the bread of hard toil;
the Lord provides as the beloved get their sleep.

See, heritage of Adonai!
Sons are a reward, and daughters of the womb.
Like arrows in the hand of a warrior,
so are children of one's youth.

Blessed are they whose quivers are full of them;
they will not be shamed
when they speak with enmity at the gate.

Glory to the *Friend* and to the *Brother* and to the *Holy Sister,*
As it was in the beginning, is now, and will be forever; Amen.

Antiphon

READING **SONG OF SONGS 8:7**

Deep waters cannot quench love, and even rivers cannot wash her away. If one were to give all the wealth the house for love, that one would be scorned and mocked.

RESPONSORY I long to gaze on you, Lord;
show me your face.

GOSPEL ANTIPHON

Virgins of the Lord,
bless the Lord for ever.

RAINBOW PRAYER

INTERCESSIONS   for the people of God; the cosmos; the poor...

CLOSING PRAYER

> Lord, the crux is your forgiving mercy.
> May we share eternal life
> in the joy of your virgins.
> Amen

OUR ABBA...

MARY SATURDAY

+ Lord, give wonder and awe
  in your presence,
  and humble clarity to trust
  what you want me to ponder.

PSALM 67

Antiphon *Lord, your salvation goes out to every nation.*

May God be gracious to us and bless us,
may God's faces shine upon us.
How else can your ways be known on the earth
and your salvation among all the nations?

May the peoples praise you, God,
may the peoples praise you, all of them.

May the nations be glad and sing for joy
for you rule the peoples
and guide nations of the earth into justice.

May the peoples praise you, God,
may the peoples praise you, all of them.

Psalm 67, continued

The land will yield her harvest, God will bless us,
and all the ends of the earth will revere our God.

Glory to the *Creator* and to the *Redeemer* and to the *Holy Breath,*
As it was in the beginning, is now, and will be forever; Amen.

Antiphon   *Lord, your salvation goes out to every nation.*

ISAIAH 2:2-5

Antiphon   *Let our song be sung to the Lord.*

In the last of the days
the mountain of Adonai's temple
will be established as chief of the mountains,
raised above the hills.

All the nations will stream to it.
Many peoples will come and say,
"Come, let us go up to the mountain of Adonai,
to the house of the God of Jacob,
who will teach us the ways
so we may walk in the path."

Indeed, from Zion the law will go out
and from Jerusalem the word of Adonai,
who will judge between the nations
and settle disputes for many peoples.

MARY - SATURDAY

They will beat their swords into plowshares
and their spears into pruning hooks.
Nations will not take up the sword against nations,
and they will train for war no more.

House of Jacob, come!
Let us walk in Adonai's light.

Glory to the *Creator* and to the *Redeemer* and to the *Holy Breath,*
As it was in the beginning, is now, and will be forever; Amen.

Antiphon

PHILIPPIANS 2:6-11

Antiphon   *In the beginning was the word,*
and the word was with God
and the word was God.

Christ Jesus, subsisting in the form of God,
did not deem equality with God
something to grab,
but emptied himself,
taking the form of a slave,
becoming in human likeness.

And being found in human fashion,
he humbled himself,
becoming obedient until death,
and death on a cross.

Philippians 2, continued

And so God highly exalted him,
and gave to him the name above every name,
that in the name of Jesus
every knee should bend,
of heavenly beings and earthly beings,
and beings under the earth;

And every tongue acknowledge
to the glory of God the Abba
that Jesus Christ is Lord.

Glory to the *Creator* and to the *Redeemer* and to the *Holy Breath*,
As it was in the beginning, is now, and will be forever; Amen.

Antiphon   *In the beginning was the word,*
and the word was with God
and the word was God.

MARY - SATURDAY

READING **GALATIANS 4:4-5**

When the fullness of time had come, God sent forth God's own Son, becoming of a woman, becoming under the law, that he might redeem those under the law, that we might receive the full adoption as heirs of God.

RESPONSORY

> Hail Mary, full of Grace, the Lord is with you.
> *Blessed are you among women,*
> *and blessed is the fruit of your womb, Jesus.*
> *Holy Mary, Mother of God, pray for us sinners,*
> *now and at the hour of our death. Amen.*

GOSPEL ANTIPHON

> *The Lord has looked with favor*
> *on the servant of the Lord;*
> *the Almighty has done great things for me.*

INTERCESSIONS   for the people of God; the cosmos; the poor…

CLOSING PRAYER

Adonai, in your plan of salvation
your Word became human, born of Mary.
May the mother of God pray for us always
in communion with all the saints. Amen.

OUR ABBA…

WORK HOURS

SUNDAY MORNING

+ Lord, let your favor shine on the work of
my mind and heart and soul and strength.

PSALM 115:1-11

Antiphon   *The living God is my strength;*
sing praise to God.

Not to us, **Adonai**, not to us,
but to your name give glory
because of your love, because of your fidelity.
Why say the nations, "Where now is their God?"

Our God now is in the heavens
and does all that God pleases.
Their idols are silver and gold,
made of human hands.

RAINBOW PRAYER

Made with a mouth, they cannot speak;
made with eyes, they cannot see;
made with ears, they cannot hear;
made with a nose, they cannot smell;

made with hands, they cannot feel;
made with feet, they cannot walk,
and they make not a sound in their throat.
Like them will become those who make them,
and all who trust in them.

Israel, trust Adonai, your help and your shield.
Aaron, trust Adonai, your help and your shield.
You who fear Adonai, trust Adonai,
your help and your shield.

Glory to the Abba and to the Son and to the Holy Spirit,
As it was in the beginning, is now, and will be forever; Amen.

Antiphon

READING **GENESIS 1:27-31**

So God created the human in God's image, created in the image of God, male and female God created them. God blessed them and God said to them, "Be fertile and multiply; fill the earth; subdue her. Rule over the fish of the sea, the birds of the air, and every living thing moving over the ground." God said, "See, I give you every seed-bearing plant that seeds the whole face of the earth and every tree

Genesis 1, continued

with fruit and seed seeding for food for you, every beast of the earth, bird of the air, thing moving on the ground with life-breath in it, and green plant for food," and it was.

God saw all that God made and found it very good. Evening and morning came, the sixth day.

RESPONSORY   I will sing for ever of your mercy, Lord;
make known to all the fidelity of God.

Lord\ *have mercy.* **Christ\ have mercy.** Lord\ have mercy.

SUNDAY AFTERNOON

+ Lord, let your favor shine on the work of
my mind and heart and soul and strength.

DANIEL 3:52-57

Antiphon   *Bless the Lord,*
all you works of the Lord.

Blessed are you, O Lord, God of our ancestors,
praiseworthy and exalted above all forever.

Blessed is your glorious and holy name,
praiseworthy and exalted above all forever.

Blessed are you in the temple of your sacred glory,
praiseworthy and exalted above all forever.

Blessed are you who sit high on the cherubim
and look into the depths,
praiseworthy and exalted above all forever.

Blessed are you on your royal throne,
praiseworthy and exalted above all forever.

Blessed are you in the dome of heaven,
to be hymned and glorified forever.

Bless the Lord, all you works of the Lord,
sing praise and high exaltation forever.

Glory to the Abba and to the Son and to the Holy Spirit,
As it was in the beginning, is now, and will be forever; Amen.

Antiphon

READING **MATTHEW 6:25-26,31-33**

And so I say to you: Do not be absorbed by your life, what you may eat or what you may drink, nor about your body, what you may put on it. Is not life more than food? The body more than clothes? Look at the birds of heaven and see that they neither sow nor reap nor gather into barns; and your heavenly Father feeds them. Are you not more excellent than them?...

So do not be absorbed with asking, 'what may

we eat' or 'what may we drink?' or 'what may we put on?' For the nations seek after all these things. Your heavenly Abba knows that you need all these things. But seek first your Abba's realm and justice, and all these things will be given to you.

RESPONSORY   I desire to live in God's holy dwelling.
My whole being rejoices in the living God.

Lord\ have mercy. **Christ\ have mercy.** *L*ord\ have mercy.

MONDAY MORNING

+ Lord, let your favor shine on the work of
my mind and heart and soul and strength.

PSALM 40:2-4,6-9

Antiphon   *Doing the will of my Abba
is the food that sustains me.*

Waiting, I waited for Adonai,
who turned to me and heard my cry,

who lifted me from the slime pit
and from the muddy mire,
and set my feet on rock,
making firm my standing place…

Adonai, my God, many are your deeds of wonder
and your plans cannot be equaled.
Should I speak and tell of them
they would be too many to declare.

Sacrifice and offerings you did not desire,
but my ears you keep open for me.
Burnt offering and sin offering you did not require.
Then I said, "Here, I have come;

in the scroll, in the book, it is written of me.
To do your will, my God, is my desire,
and your law is within my heart."

Glory to the Abba and to the Son and to the Holy Spirit,
As it was in the beginning, is now, and will be forever; Amen.

Antiphon

READING **DEUTERONOMY 10:12-13**

And now, Israel, what does your God Adonai ask from you? But only to fear Adonai your God, to walk in all your God's ways, to love and serve Adonai your God with all your heart and with all your soul, and to observe Adonai's commands and decrees that I give you this day for your own good.

RESPONSORY Claim me again as your own, Lord,
and have mercy on me.

Lord\ have mercy. **Christ\ have mercy.** Lord\ have mercy.

MONDAY AFTERNOON

+ Lord, let your favor shine on the work of
  my mind and heart and soul and strength.

PSALM 119:129-136

Antiphon   *Lord, guide my steps by your word.*

Your statutes are wonderful;
I myself obey them.
Your words enter giving light
and understanding to the simple.

I open my mouth and breathe heavy,
longing for your commands.
Turn to me and have mercy
as is your custom with lovers of your name.

Direct my footsteps by your word;
prevent sin from ruling over me.
Redeem me from human oppression
that I may obey your precepts.

Shine your faces on your servant
and teach me your decrees.
Streams of tears flow down my eyes
over disobedience to your teaching.

WORK HOURS

Glory to the Abba and to the Son and to the Holy Spirit,
As it was in the beginning, is now, and will be forever; Amen.

Antiphon

READING   **1 CORINTHIANS 12:24b-26**

God put together the body, giving more abundant honor to the member lacking it, lest there be division in the body, and so the same members give care on behalf of one another. Whenever one member suffers, all the members suffer with it. Whenever one is honored, all rejoice with that one.

RESPONSORY

> Lord, gather your people from all the nations
> *that we may give your name the glory.*

Lord\ have mercy.
Christ\ have mercy.
Lord\ have mercy.

TUESDAY MORNING

+ Lord, let your favor shine on the work of
  my mind and heart and soul and strength.

PSALM 119:1-8

Antiphon   *They are happy who live by God's law.*

Blessed are people blameless on the way,
who walk by your teaching, Adonai.
Blessed are keepers of your statutes
who seek with all their heart.

They do no wrong;
they walk in the way.
You laid down your precepts
to be obeyed with care.

Oh that my ways were steadfast
in obedience to your decrees!
Then I will have no shame
when pondering all your commands.

I will praise you with a sincere heart
so to learn your justice.
I will obey your decrees;
do not forsake me.

Glory to the Abba and to the Son and to the Holy Spirit,
As it was in the beginning, is now, and will be forever; Amen.

Antiphon

READING   **JEREMIAH 31:31-33**

"See, days are coming," declares Adonai, "when I will make a new covenant with the house of Israel and with the house of Judah, not like the covenant I made with their ancestors on the day I took them by the hand to lead them out from the land of Egypt. My covenant they broke, though I made them my spouse," declares Adonai.

"But this is the covenant that I will make with the house of Israel after those days," declares Adonai. "I will put my law in their mind, and I will write it on their heart, and I will be their God, and they will be my people."

RESPONSORY   Create in me a clean heart, O God;
do not send me away from your face.

Lord\ have mercy.
Christ\ have mercy.
Lord\ have mercy.

TUESDAY AFTERNOON

+ Lord, let your favor shine on the work of
my mind and heart and soul and strength.

ISAIAH 55:10-11

Antiphon *Let the clouds rain down the just one
and earth bring forth a savior.*

As the rain and the snow
come down from the heavens
and do not return there
without first watering the earth

making her bud fertile and flourish,
yielding seed to the sower
and bread to the eater,
so is the word that goes out from my mouth.

My word will not return to me empty
but will accomplish what I desire
and will achieve the purpose
for which I sent it.

Glory to the Abba and to the Son and to the Holy Spirit,
As it was in the beginning, is now, and will be forever; Amen.

Antiphon

WORK HOURS 73

READING   **1 JOHN 3:17-18**

Whoever has the means to live in the world and beholds a sibling in need and closes off all feelings of compassion, how can the love of God abide in that one? Little children, let us love, not in word or speech, but in work and truth.

RESPONSORY   Happy the compassionate thoughtful;
their memory will be cherished.

Lord\ have mercy. **Christ\ have mercy**. Lord\ have mercy.

WEDNESDAY MORNING

+ Lord, let your favor shine on the work of
my mind and heart and soul and strength.

PSALM 90

Antiphon   *May the favor of the Lord rest upon us
and make good the work of our hands.*

You, Lord, you have been our refuge
from generation to generation.
Before the mountains were born,
before you brought forth earth,
from eternity to eternity, you are God.

Psalm 90, continued

You turn humans back to dust and say,
"Return, sons and daughters of humanity."
A thousand years in your eyes
are like the day yesterday that went by,
like one watch of the night.

You sweep humans into the sleep
like new grass in the morning that sprouts:
in the morning it springs up and sprouts
and then by the evening is withered and dry.

Indeed we can be consumed in your anger
and terrified by your indignation.
You set our iniquities before you,
our secrets in the light of your presences.

Indeed all our days pass away under your anger;
we finish our years like a sigh.
Our days last for seventy years
or eighty if given the strength.

The best part of them are trouble and sorrow,
passing quickly, and we fly away.
Who knows the power of your anger,
who fears your wrath?

Number our days aright;
teach, that we may gain hearts of wisdom.
How long, Adonai, until you relent?
Have compassion on your servants.

WORK HOURS

Satisfy our morning hunger
with your unfailing love
that we may sing for joy and be glad all our days.
Make us glad, equal to our affliction,
the years of trouble we have seen.

May your deeds be shown to your servants
and your splendor to their children.
May the favor of the Lord our God rest upon us
and the work of our hands be made good;
yes, make good the work of our hands.

Glory to the Abba and to the Son and to the Holy Spirit,
As it was in the beginning, is now, and will be forever; Amen.

Antiphon   *May the favor of the Lord rest upon us
and make good the work of our hands.*

READING   **MATTHEW 11:28-30**

Come to me, all who labor and carry burdens, and I will rest you. Take my yoke upon you and learn from me, because I am meek and humble of heart, and you will find rest for your soul, for my yoke is easy, and my burden is light.

RESPONSORY   Lord, my inheritance and my cup,
my life is in your hands.

Lord\ have mercy. **Christ\ have mercy**. Lord\ have mercy.

WEDNESDAY AFTERNOON

+ Lord, let your favor shine on the work of
my mind and heart and soul and strength.

PSALM 128

Antiphon   *Walk in the ways of the Lord.*

Blessed are all who fear Adonai
and walk in the way.

Indeed you will eat from the labor of your hands.
To you will be blessings and prosperity,
and your spouse like a fruitful vine
inside and outside your house,
sons and daughters around your table
like shoots of the olives.

See: one who fears Adonai is blessed;
may Adonai bless you from Zion.
See and enjoy the prosperity of Jerusalem
all the days of your life,
and the joy of the children of your children.

Peace be upon Israel.

Glory to the Abba and to the Son and to the Holy Spirit,
As it was in the beginning, is now, and will be forever; Amen.

Antiphon

READING **1 CORINTHIANS 13:4-9,13**

Love *(agape)* is patient; love is kind. It is not jealous; love does not boast. It is not puffed up, arrogant, rude, or self-seeking. It is not provoked, does not reckon wrongdoings, and does not rejoice in bad things, but rejoices with the truth. Love covers all things, believes all things, hopes all things, endures all things.

Love never fails. Prophecies will be abolished, tongues will cease, and knowledge will be abolished; for we know in part and we prophesy in part... But now remain faith, hope, love, these three; and the greatest of these is love.

RESPONSORY

> All who seek you, Lord, will dance for joy;
> *they will proclaim your greatness to forever.*

Lord\ have mercy.
Christ\ have mercy.
Lord\ have mercy.

THURSDAY MORNING

+ Lord, let your favor shine on the work of
my mind and heart and soul and strength.

PSALM 104:1-15

Antiphon *The Lord brings forth bread from the earth and wine to warm the human heart.*

Soul of me, praise Adonai!
My God, Adonai, you are beyond measure.
Splendor and majesty clothe you,
wrapped in light as a garment,

stretching out over the heavens like a tent,
laying beams on the waters of the upper chambers.
You make a chariot of the clouds,
riding on wings of wind,
making messengers of the winds
and servants of flaming fire.

You have set foundations on earth,
unmoveable for ever and ever.
Deep is your garment, covering the earth;
above the mountains the waters stood.

At your rebuke, they then fled;
at the sound of your thunder they took flight.
They flowed over mountains
and went down into valleys
to the places you assigned for them.
You set a boundary they are not to cross;
never again are they to cover the earth.

You make springs of water pour into ravines;
between the mountains they flow.
They give drink to all beasts of the field;
they quench the thirst of donkeys.
Birds of the air nest in branches beside them;
they give you their song.

You water mountains from your upper chambers;
by the fruit of your works the earth is satisfied.
You make grass grow for the cattle
and plants for human beings to cultivate

to bring forth food from the earth,
wine to make glad the human heart,
oil to make faces shine,
and bread to sustain the human heart.

Glory to the Abba and to the Son and to the Holy Spirit,
As it was in the beginning, is now, and will be forever; Amen.

Antiphon

READING **1 JOHN 4:9-11**

By this God's love was shown to us: God sent God's only begotten Son into the world, that we might live through him. In this is love; not that we have loved God, but that God loved us and sent the Son as expiation for our sins. Beloved, as God so loved us, we also ought to love one another.

RESPONSORY Look on us, O strong protector,
and see the face of your Christ.

Lord\ have mercy.
Christ\ have mercy.
Lord\ have mercy.

THURSDAY AFTERNOON

+ Lord, let your favor shine on the work of
my mind and heart and soul and strength.

PSALM 104:16-30

Antiphon *The Lord looked upon all creation
and saw that it was very good.*

They are all Adonai's well watered trees,
cedars of Lebanon planted
where birds make their nests,
and the pine tree where the stork makes a home,
mountains, the high ones, for wild goats,
and crags, a refuge for rock badgers.

You made the moon to mark off seasons
and the sun that knows when to set.
You bring darkness
and all beasts of the forest prowl in the night.
The lions roar for prey
seeking their food from God.

The sun rises, they steal away,
and into their dens they lie down.
Human beings go out to do their work
and labor until the evening.

Psalm 104, continued

How varied are your works, Adonai!
All of them in wisdom you made.
The earth is full of your creatures.

There is the sea, vast and spacious;
living creatures countless there,
small ones and large ones.
There ships go about
and leviathan which you formed for frolic.

All of them look to you
to give them food at their time.
You give to them and they gather,
you open your hands
and they are goodly satisfied.

You hide your face and they are lost,
you take away their breath and they die
and to their dust they return.
You breathe your Spirit, and they are created,
and you renew the faces of earth.

Glory to the Abba and to the Son and to the Holy Spirit,
As it was in the beginning, is now, and will be forever; Amen.

Antiphon *The Lord looked upon all creation*
and saw that it was very good.

WORK HOURS

READING **MARK 6:1-3a**

And Jesus went forth from there and came into his native place, and his disciples followed him. And when a sabbath came, he began to teach in the synagogue, and the many hearing were astonished, saying, "Where did this human get these things? And what is this wisdom given to him? And how are such powerful deeds coming about through these hands? Is this human not the carpenter, son of Mary and brother of James and Joses and Judas and Simon? And are not his sisters here with us?"

RESPONSORY

> Bless the Lord, all you works of the Lord;
> *give praise and glory to forever.*

Lord\ have mercy. **Christ\ have mercy.** Lord\ have mercy.

FRIDAY MORNING

+ Lord, let your favor shine on the work of my mind and heart and soul and strength.

PSALM 80

Antiphon   *God of Hosts, look now from heaven!*
See and watch over the vine you planted!

Psalm 80

Hear us, One Shepherd of Israel,
you who lead Joseph like a flock.
From your throne on the cherubim, shine forth
before Ephraim, Benjamin and Manasseh!
Awaken your might! Come to our salvation!

O God, restore us!
Make your faces shine that we may be saved!

Until when, Adonai, God of Hosts,
will you smolder against
the prayer of your people?
You fed them with bread of tears
and you made them drink tears by the bowlful.
You made us a contention to our neighbors,
and enmity mocks us.

God of Hosts, restore us!
Make your faces shine that we may be saved!

Out from Egypt, you brought a vine;
you drove out the nations and you planted it.
You cleared the ground before her;
her roots took root and she filled the land.

Mountains were covered by her shade
and the mighty cedars by her branches.
She sent out her branches to the Sea,
and her shoots as far as the River.

Why have you broken down her walls?
All who pass by the way pluck her fruit.
The boar from the forest ravages her,
and creatures of the field feed on her.

God of Hosts, return now!
Look down from heaven!
See and watch over this vine,
this root that your right hand planted.
Some would burn it or cut it down;
at the rebuke of your faces may those plans perish.

Let your hand be on the one at your right hand,
the descendant of Adam you raised up for yourself.
Then we will not turn away from you;
you revive us and we will call on your name.

Adonai, God of Hosts, restore us!
Make your faces shine that we may be saved!

Glory to the Abba and to the Son and to the Holy Spirit,
As it was in the beginning, is now, and will be forever; Amen.

Antiphon   *God of Hosts, look now from heaven!*
See and watch over the vine you planted!

READING   **EPHESIANS 2:8-10**

By grace you have been saved through faith, and this is not from you; it is the gift of God; not from works, so no one should boast. For we are the handiwork of God, created in Christ Jesus for the good works God has prepared in advance, that in them we might walk.

RESPONSORY

> Lord, make known your way to us on earth;
> *may all nations know you as their Savior.*

Lord\ have mercy. **Christ\ have mercy.** Lord\ have mercy.

FRIDAY AFTERNOON

+ Lord, let your favor shine on the work of
   my mind and heart and soul and strength.

PSALM 133

Antiphon   *The multitude of believers*
                 was of one mind and heart.

See how good and how pleasant it is
to live as siblings
dwelling in unity.

> Like the precious oil
> running down on the head
> and on the beard of Aaron,
> running down on his collar and robes,
>
> as if the dew of Hermon
> was falling on Mount Zion,
> there Adonai bestows
> the blessing of life to forever.

Glory to the Abba and to the Son and to the Holy Spirit,
As it was in the beginning, is now, and will be forever; Amen.

Antiphon

READING **WISDOM 1:13-15**

God did not make death, and God does not delight in the death of the living. God created all things that they might have being; the generative forces of the world are wholesome, and there is no destructive drug among them, and the dominion of Hades is not on earth. For justice is undying.

RESPONSORY   With the Lord there is mercy
and fullness of redemption.

Lord\ have mercy.
Christ\ have mercy.
Lord\ have mercy.

SATURDAY MORNING

+ Lord, let your favor shine on the work of
  my mind and heart and soul and strength.

PSALM 92:1-9,11,13-16

Antiphon *In the morning we sing of your mercy, Lord,
and at night of your fidelity.*

It is good to praise Adonai,
to make music to your name, Most High,
to proclaim your love in the morning
and your fidelity at night
on the ten-string and on the lyre,
and the melody of the harp.

For you make me glad by your deeds, Adonai;
at the works of your hands I sing for joy.
How great are your works, Adonai;
very profound are your thoughts.
The senseless human does not know
and the fool does not understand.

Though the bad can spring up like grass
and doers of the bad seem to flourish,
their ways will be destroyed to forever.
But you, Adonai, are on high to forever…

WORK HOURS

> You gave me strength like a wild ox
> and I was anointed with fresh oil…
> The just will flourish like the palm tree,
> and grow like a cedar of Lebanon.
>
> Planted in the house of Adonai,
> in the courts of our God they will flourish.
> In old age they will still bear fruit,
> ever full of sap and still green,
> to proclaim, "Adonai is just,
> in my Rock there is no wrong."

Glory to the Abba and to the Son and to the Holy Spirit,
As it was in the beginning, is now, and will be forever; Amen.

Antiphon

READING   **JEREMIAH 6:16a**

This Adonai says, "Stand at the crossroads; look and ask for the ancient paths, where the good way is; walk in her, and find rest for your soul."

RESPONSORY   Your words are my eternal heritage;
                          they are the joy of my heart.

Lord\ have mercy.
Christ\ have mercy.
Lord\ have mercy.

SATURDAY AFTERNOON

+ Lord, let your favor shine on the work of
   my mind and heart and soul and strength.

PSALM 34:1-11

Antiphon   *Look to the Lord and be enlightened.*

I will extol Adonai at all times,
praise always on my lips.
My soul she will boast in Adonai,
let afflicted ones hear and let them rejoice.

Glorify Adonai with me!
Let us exalt the name together.
I sought Adonai, who answered me
and delivered me from all my fears.

They look to the Name and are radiant;
their faces are never covered with shame.
Adonai heard this poor human call
and saved me from all the troubles.

An angel encamps around
and delivers all who fear Adonai.
Taste and see that Adonai is good!
Blessed is the one who takes this refuge.

WORK HOURS

Fear Adonai, you saints;
for those who do so there is no lack.
Lions may grow weak and may grow hungry,
but seekers of Adonai lack no good thing.

Glory to the Abba and to the Son and to the Holy Spirit,
As it was in the beginning, is now, and will be forever; Amen.

Antiphon

READING   **MICAH 6:8**

Adonai has shown you, human, what is good and what Adonai requires of you:
> To do justice,
> love kindness, and
> walk humbly with your God.

RESPONSORY

> All your commands are a joy to me, Lord;
> *never shall I forget your word.*

Lord\ have mercy.
Christ\ have mercy.
Lord\ have mercy.

IN HEALTH & IN HEALING

SUNDAY MORNING

+ Abba, thank you…
Lord Jesus, bless us with mercy…
Holy Spirit, help…

PSALM 100

Antiphon   *May my song before the Lord be one of joy.*

Shout for joy to Adonai, all you earth!
Serve Adonai with gladness!
Come into the presence with joyful song.

RAINBOW PRAYER

Know that Adonai is God, who made us,
whose people we are,
in whose pasture we are the sheep.

Enter the gates with thanksgiving,
go into the courts with praise!
Give thanks and give praise to the Name!

Good is Adonai, and loving to forever,
and faithful through generations and generation.

Glory to the Abba and to the Son and to the Holy Breath,
As it was in the beginning, is now, and will be forever; Amen.

Antiphon

READING   **MARK 16:5-6**

And entering into the tomb they saw a young man sitting on the right clothed in a white robe, and they were greatly astonished. He said to them, "Be not greatly astonished. Jesus you seek, the Nazarene who was crucified; he has been raised, he is not here. Behold: the place where they put him."

RESPONSORY   All of creation proclaims
                             the greatness of your glory.

Let us bless the Lord/.
R. **Thanks be to God/.**

SUNDAY EVENING

+ Abba, thank you...
  Lord Jesus, bless us with mercy...
  Holy Spirit, help...

PSALM 23

Antiphon
*The Lord has brought me
to pastures alive and green.*

Adonai is my shepherd; nothing do I lack.
My Lord lays me down in green pastures
and leads me beside still quiet waters,
restoring my soul and guiding me
in paths of justice for the Lord's own namesake.

So when I walk in the deep dark valley
I will not fear for you are with me,
your rod and staff a comfort to me.

A table you prepare before me
in the presence even of enmity.
My head you anoint with oil
and my cup is overflowing.

IN HEALTH & IN HEALING

> Surely goodness and love will follow me
> all the days of my life
> and I will dwell in the Lord's own house
> for length of days.

Glory to the Abba and to the Son and to the Holy Breath,
As it was in the beginning, is now, and will be forever; Amen.

Antiphon

READING   **1 CORINTHIANS 15:3-8**

For I handed on to you among the first things what I also received, that Christ died on behalf of our sins, according to the scriptures, and that he was buried, and that he was raised on the third day, according to the scriptures, and that he showed himself to Cephas, then to the twelve.

Afterward he showed himself to over five hundred brothers and sisters at one time, of whom the majority remain until now, though some have fallen asleep. Afterward he showed himself to James, then to all the apostles, and last of all, even as if to one aborted, he showed himself also to me.

RESPONSORY   Lord Jesus Christ, Son of the living God,
                     have mercy on us.

Let us bless the Lord/.
R. **Thanks be to God/.**

MONDAY MORNING

+ Abba, thank you…
  Lord Jesus, bless us with mercy…
  Holy Spirit, help…

PSALM 43

Antiphon *Let anyone who is thirsty
come to me and drink.*

God, vindicate me;
plead my cause against an ungodly nation;
rescue me from humans deceitful doing the bad.

God, my strength, why am I rejected?
Why must I go about mourning,
oppressed by enmity?

Send forth your light and your fidelity;
let them guide me to your dwellings
and bring me to your holy mountain.

Then I will go to the altar of God,
to El, my joy and delight,
and I will praise you with harp, God, my God.

Why are you downcast, my soul?
Why are you disturbed within me?
Put hope in God, whom I will yet praise,
the saving help of my face, my God.

Glory to the Abba and to the Son and to the Holy Breath,
As it was in the beginning, is now, and will be forever; Amen.

Antiphon

READING   **MATTHEW 8:1-3**

As Jesus came down from the mountain, crowds of many followed him. Behold a leper approached and worshipped him saying, "Lord, if you are willing you are able to cleanse me." Stretching out his hand he touched him saying, "I am willing; be cleansed." Right away the leprosy was cleansed from him.

RESPONSORY   All of creation proclaims
the greatness of your glory.

Let us bless the Lord/.
R. **Thanks be to God/.**

MONDAY EVENING

+ Abba, thank you…
Lord Jesus, bless us with mercy…
Holy Spirit, help…

PSALM 121

Antiphon *My help is from the Lord, watch over me;*
the Maker of heaven and earth is my guardian.

I lift up my eyes to the mountains.
From where does my help come?
My help comes from Adonai,
Maker of heavens and earth,

who will not let your foot slip
nor slumber when guarding you.
Indeed the guardian of Israel
will not slumber and will not sleep.

Adonai is your guardian,
the Most High at your right hand.
By day the sun will not harm you,
nor the moon by the night.

IN HEALTH & IN HEALING

> Adonai will keep you from all harm
> and guard your life.
> Adonai will guard your going and coming
> from now and to forevermore.

Glory to the Abba and to the Son and to the Holy Breath,
As it was in the beginning, is now, and will be forever; Amen.

Antiphon

READING   **EZEKIEL 36:24-26**

I will take you out of the nations and I will gather you from all of the countries, and I will bring you back into your land. I will sprinkle on you clean waters, and you will be clean from all of your impurities, and from all of your idols I will cleanse you. I will give to you a new heart and I will put inside of you a new spirit, and I will remove the heart of stone from your flesh and I will give to you a heart of flesh.

RESPONSORY   Blessed be the Lord our God,
blessed from age to age.

Let us bless the Lord/.
R. **Thanks be to God/.**

TUESDAY MORNING

+ Abba, thank you…
  Lord Jesus, bless us with mercy…
  Holy Spirit, help…

PSALM 139:1-10,23-24

Antiphon   *How precious to me, Lord,
                 are your thoughts.*

Adonai, you search me and you know me.
You know my sitting and my rising;
you perceive my thoughts from afar.
You mark my going and my lying down,
and you are familiar with all of my ways.

When a word is not yet on my tongue
you see it, Adonai; you know them all.
Behind and before you hem me in
and rest your hand upon me.
Too wonderful for me is this knowledge,
more lofty than what I can attain.

Where can I hide from your Spirit?
Where could I flee from your presences?
If I go up to the heavens, you are there;
if I make a bed in Sheol, you I see!

IN HEALTH & IN HEALING

If I rise on the wings of dawn,
if I settle on the far side of the sea,
even there your hand will guide me
and your right hand will hold me…

Search me, El, and know my heart!
Test me, and know my anxious thoughts!
See if there is in me an offensive way,
then lead me in the way everlasting!

Glory to the Abba and to the Son and to the Holy Breath,
As it was in the beginning, is now, and will be forever; Amen.

Antiphon

READING **MARK 3:1-5**

Jesus again entered into a synagogue. There was there a man with a hand that had been withered. They watched him carefully whether he would heal him on the sabbath, that they might accuse him. He said to the man with the dry hand, "Rise into the midst." And he asked them, "Is it lawful to do good on the sabbath or to do evil, to save life or to kill?" They were silent. Looking round on them with anger, being very grieved at the hardness of their heart, he said to the man, "Stretch forth the hand." He stretched forth and his hand was restored.

RESPONSORY My God stands by me;
in God is all my trust.

Let us bless the Lord/. R. **Thanks be to God**/.

TUESDAY EVENING

+ Abba, thank you…
   Lord Jesus, bless us with mercy…
   Holy Spirit, help…

PSALM 84:2-10

Antiphon   *Blessed are they who dwell in your house,
my Ruler and my God.*

How lovely are your dwellings,
Adonai Sabaoth!
My soul she yearns and even faints
for the courts of Adonai;
my heart and my flesh cry out for God alive.

Even the sparrow found a home
and the swallow a nest for her
where she may settle her young ones
near your altar, Adonai Sabaoth,
my Ruler and my God.

Blessed are the dwellers in your house,
ever they praise you.
Blessed are the ones whose strength is in you,
who make a pilgrimage in their hearts.

IN HEALTH & IN HEALING

> Passing through the Baca Valley,
> springs are found,
> pools covered over with autumn rains.
> They go from strength to strength
> and appear before God in Zion.
>
> Adonai, God Sabaoth, hear my prayer!
> Listen, God of Jacob. God, our shield, look!
> Look on the face of your anointed one!

Glory to the Abba and to the Son and to the Holy Breath,
As it was in the beginning, is now, and will be forever; Amen.

Antiphon

READING **2 CORINTHIANS 12:14b**

> I do not seek your things,
> what you have,
> but you…

RESPONSORY Through all eternity, Lord,
your promise stands unshaken.

Let us bless the Lord/.
R. **Thanks be to God/.**

WEDNESDAY MORNING

+ Abba, thank you…
   Lord Jesus, bless us with mercy…
   Holy Spirit, help…

PSALM 19:1-7

Antiphon   *The heavens declare the glory of God.*

The heavens declare the glory of God,
and the sky proclaims the work of God's hands.
Day after day, speech pouring forth,
knowledge is on display night after night.

There is no speech, there is no language,
and no sound is heard.
Yet into all the earth their line goes out
and their words to the ends of the world.

There God has pitched a tent for the sun,
and like a bridegroom coming forth,
and like an athlete running the course,
rejoices.

Glory to the Abba and to the Son and to the Holy Breath,
As it was in the beginning, is now, and will be forever; Amen.

Antiphon

IN HEALTH & IN HEALING

READING   **ROMANS 8:22-27**

We know that all creation groans together, in pain as in labor, until now. And not only this, but we ourselves, the firstfruit of the Spirit, groan within ourselves as we eagerly expect our adoption, the redemption of our bodies. For by hope we were saved; but hope that is seen is not hope, for why would anyone hope for what is seen? But if we hope for what we do not see, through patience we eagerly wait.

And similarly also the Spirit shares in our weakness. For we do not know how to pray as is fitting, but the Spirit prays on our behalf with inexpressible groanings. And the one searching our heart knows what is the mind of the Spirit, because the Spirit intercedes on behalf of saints according to the will of God.

RESPONSORY   Attract my heart to your will, O God;
draw my feet to your way.

Let us bless the Lord/.
R. **Thanks be to God/.**

WEDNESDAY EVENING

+ Abba, thank you…
Lord Jesus, bless us with mercy…
Holy Spirit, help…

PSALM 131

Antiphon *Unless you become as a child
you will not enter the realm of God.*

Adonai, my heart is not proud
and my eyes are not haughty
and I am not busied with the great matters,
with things so wonderful as to be beyond me.

But indeed I have become still
and quiet in my soul
like a child with a mother, being weaned.
Like one being weaned is my soul within me.

Israel, put your hope in Adonai
from now and to forevermore.

Glory to the Abba and to the Son and to the Holy Breath,
As it was in the beginning, is now, and will be forever; Amen.

Antiphon

IN HEALTH & IN HEALING

READING   **COLOSSIANS 1:12-20**

Give joyful thanks to the Abba who made you fit
for your part of the lot of the saints in light,
who delivered us out of the authority of darkness,
transitioning us into the realm of the beloved Son
in whom we have redemption,
the forgiveness of our sins.
The Son is the image of the invisible God,
the firstborn of all creation.
In him all things were created,
in the heavens and on the earth,
the visible and the invisible,
whether thrones, lordships, rulers or authorities.
All creation has come to be through and for him.
He is before all things,
and in him all things hold together.
He is the head of the body, the church,
and the beginning, the firstborn from the dead,
so that in all things he may hold the first place.
In him all the fullness was well pleased to dwell,
and through him reconciliation to himself
of all things on earth and things in the heavens,
making peace through the blood of his cross.

RESPONSORY   Claim me again, Lord, as your very own
                      and show me your mercy.

Let us bless the Lord/.   R. **Thanks be to God**/.

THURSDAY MORNING

+ Abba, thank you...
   Lord Jesus, bless us with mercy...
   Holy Spirit, help...

PSALM 86:1-7,11

Antiphon *Bring joy to me, your servant,*
for to you, Lord, I lift up my soul.

Hear in your ear, Adonai;
answer me for I am poor and needy.
Guard my life for I am devoted;
save your servant, my God,
the one trusting in you.

Have mercy on me, Lord,
for to you I call all the day.
Bring joy to your servant,
for to you, Lord, I lift up my soul.

Indeed, Lord, you are kind and forgiving
and abundant in love for all who call to you.
Hear my prayer, Adonai;
listen to the sound of my cries for mercy.

IN HEALTH & IN HEALING

> In the day of my trouble I will call to you
> for you will answer me…
>
> Teach me, Adonai, your way
> and I will walk in your truth.
> Undivide my heart
> that I may fear your name.

Glory to the Abba and to the Son and to the Holy Breath,
As it was in the beginning, is now, and will be forever; Amen.

Antiphon

READING **ROMANS 8:14-17**

As many as are led by the Spirit of God, these are children of God. For you did not receive a spirit of slavery, for fear again, but you received a spirit of adoption, by which we cry, "Abba, Father."

That very Spirit gives witness to our spirit that we are children of God. And if children, then also heirs, heirs on one hand of God, joint heirs on the other of Christ, since we suffer with him in order that we may also be glorified with him.

RESPONSORY   From deep in my heart I cry out to you;
Lord, hear me.

Let us bless the Lord/.
R. **Thanks be to God/.**

THURSDAY EVENING

+ Abba, thank you…
Lord Jesus, bless us with mercy…
Holy Spirit, help…

PSALM 91

Antiphon *Have no fear by day or by night;
rest in the shade of the Almighty.*

One who dwells in the shelter of Elyon,
in the shadow of Shaddai, will find rest.
I will say of Adonai, my refuge, my fortress:
in my God do I trust.

Surely the Lord will save you
from fowler snare, from deadly pestilence.
With the feather of the Lord you will be covered,
and under those wings you will find refuge,
shield and rampart, the fidelity of the Lord.

You will have no fear of terror at night
nor of arrows flying by day,
of pestilence stalking in the darkness,
nor of plague that destroys at midday.

A thousand may fall at your side,
and ten thousand at your right hand;
near to you they will not come.

Observe with your eyes, simply watch;
punishment of doers of the bad you will see.
Make Adonai, who is my refuge,
make Elyon your dwelling.

Harm will not befall you,
nor will disaster come near your tent.
God's own Angels, the Lord will command
to guard you in all of your ways.

In their hands they will lift you up;
your foot will not strike against the stone.
Upon lion and cobra you will tread,
you will trample the great lion and serpent.

"Because you love me, I will rescue you,
I will protect all who know my Name.
You will call upon me and I will answer.
I am with you in trouble;
I will deliver you and honor you.

In length of days I will satisfy you,
and show you my salvation."

Glory to the Abba and to the Son and to the Holy Breath,
As it was in the beginning, is now, and will be forever; Amen.

Antiphon

READING **LUKE 6:17-19**

Jesus came down with the disciples and the chosen Twelve and stood on a level place, and a multitude of many people from all Judea and Jerusalem and the coast country of Tyre and Sidon came to hear him and to be healed from their diseases; and those tormented by unclean spirits were cured. All in the crowd sought to touch him, because power went forth from him and healed them all.

RESPONSORY God has given us food,
bread of finest wheat.

Let us bless the Lord/.
R. **Thanks be to God/.**

FRIDAY MORNING

+ Abba, thank you…
  Lord Jesus, bless us with mercy…
  Holy Spirit, help…

PSALM 51:6,7,10-17

Antiphon *A heart that is humble
you will not send away.*

Surely, God, you desire truth in our inner parts;
in my inmost place you teach me wisdom.
You cleanse me with hyssop and I will be clean;
you wash me and I will be whiter than snow…

A clean heart create in me, God!
Renew inside me a spirit to be steadfast.
Do not cast me from your presences,
nor take from me your Holy Spirit.

Restore to me the joy of your salvation
and sustain in me a willing spirit.
I will teach transgressors your ways
and sinners will turn back to you.

Psalm 51, continued

Save me from bloodguilt, God,
God of my salvation;
my tongue will sing of your justice.
Lord, open my lips
and my mouth will proclaim your praise.

Sacrifices give you no delight;
I could bring a burnt offering,
but it would give you no pleasure.
The sacrifices, God, you will not despise
are a broken spirit and a contrite heart.

Glory to the Abba and to the Son and to the Holy Breath,
As it was in the beginning, is now, and will be forever; Amen.

Antiphon *A heart that is humble
you will not send away.*

READING **LUKE 17:20-21**

Questioned by the Pharisees about when the reign of God would come, Jesus answered them and said, "The reign of God is not coming with observation, nor will they say, 'Look, here it is,' or, 'There it is, look,' for the reign of God is within you.

RESPONSORY At break of day be merciful to me;
show me the way you want me to walk.

Let us bless the Lord/. R. **Thanks be to God**/.

FRIDAY EVENING

+ Abba, thank you…
   Lord Jesus, bless us with mercy…
   Holy Spirit, help…

PSALM 65:4,9-13

Antiphon *For you, O God, silence,
and praise in Zion.*

Blessed are the ones you choose
and bring near to live in your courts.
We are filled with the goodness of your house
and the holiness of your temple…

You care for the land and water her;
with an abundance you enrich her.
God's stream is as you ordain the earth:
filled with waters, providing grain.
You drench its furrows and level its ridges;
you soften her with showers and bless the crops.

You crown the year with your bounty;
paths overflow with your abundance.
The desert grasslands are overflowing
and the hills are clothed with gladness.

Psalm 65, continued

> The meadows are covered with the flock
> and valleys are coated with grain.
> They shout for joy; for joy they sing.

Glory to the Abba and to the Son and to the Holy Breath,
As it was in the beginning, is now, and will be forever; Amen.

Antiphon *For you, O God, silence,
and praise in Zion.*

READING **JOHN 14:1-7**

"Do not let your heart be troubled; believe in God, believe also in me. In the Abba's house there are many abodes. If not I would have told you, because I go to prepare a place for you. And if I go and prepare a place for you, I will come again and receive you to myself, that where I am you also may be. And where I go, you know the way."

Thomas said to him, "Lord, we do not know where you are going; how do we know the way?"

Jesus said to him, "I am the way and the truth and the life. No one comes to the Abba except through me. If you have known me, you have also known my Abba, whom you now know and have seen."

RESPONSORY Christ gave Christself completely for us
and rose in the power of the Spirit.

Let us bless the Lord/. R. **Thanks be to God**/.

SATURDAY MORNING

+ Abba, thank you…
Lord Jesus, bless us with mercy…
Holy Spirit, help…

PSALM 46

Antiphon   *The Lord of Hosts is with us.*

God is our refuge and strength,
our help in troubles, ever present.
And so we will not fear,
even if earth were to give way,
even if mountains were to fall
into the heart of the sea,
even if sea waters foam
or mountains quake with their surging.

River streams make glad the city of God,
the holy dwelling place of the Most High.
God is inside her and she will not fall.
God will help her at break of day.
Nations are in uproar and realms fall;
the earth melts at the voice of God.

SATURDAY MORNING, continued
Psalm 46, continued

Adonai Sabaoth is with us;
the God of Jacob is our fortress.

Come and see the works of Adonai,
the desolations brought on the earth:
making wars to cease to the ends of the earth,
breaking the bow and shattering the spear
and burning with fire the chariot and shield.

"Be still! And know that I am God.
I will be exalted among the nations;
I will be exalted on the earth."

Adonai Sabaoth is with us;
the God of Jacob is our fortress.

Glory to the Abba and to the Son and to the Holy Breath,
As it was in the beginning, is now, and will be forever; Amen.

Antiphon   *The Lord of Hosts is with us.*

READING   **EPHESIANS 3:16-22**

I pray that the Abba may give to you according to the riches of glory, by the power of the Spirit, to become strong in your inner humanity, that Christ may dwell in your hearts through faith, being rooted and founded in love, that you may have strength to comprehend with all the saints what is the breadth and length and height and depth, to know the love of Christ that excels knowledge, that you may be filled with the fullness of God.

Now to the one who by the power operating in us is able to do superabundantly beyond all things we could ask or think, to him be the glory in the church and in Christ Jesus to all generations of the eon and of the eons. Amen.

RESPONSORY You, Lord, are my refuge and strength,
all I desire in the land of the living.

Let us bless the Lord/.
R. **Thanks be to God/.**

SATURDAY EVENING

+ Abba, thank you…
  Lord Jesus, bless us with mercy…
  Holy Spirit, help…

PSALM 147:1-11

Antiphon *Let us praise the Lord with joy.*

Hallelujah!
How good it is to sing praise to our God!
How pleasant and fitting to give praise!

Adonai rebuilds Jerusalem, gathers Israel's exiles,
heals broken hearts and binds up wounds,
determines the number of the stars,
and calls to each of them by name.

Great and mighty in power is our Lord,
with unlimited understanding.
Adonai sustains the humble
and throws doers of the bad to the dust.
Sing to Adonai with thanksgiving!

Make music on the harp to our God,
who covers the skies with clouds
and supplies rain to the earth,
making grass to grow on the mountains, - -

providing food for cattle
and young ravens when they call.

Adonai finds pleasure
not in the strength of the horse
nor delight in the legs of the human,
but is delighting in those who fear Adonai
who hope in this unfailing love.

Glory to the Abba and to the Son and to the Holy Breath,
As it was in the beginning, is now, and will be forever; Amen.

Antiphon

READING **MATTHEW 8:23-27**

As Jesus got into the boat, his disciples followed him. Behold: there was a mega storm in the sea, so that the boat was swept over by the waves. But he was asleep. They approached him and woke him up saying, "Lord, save us! We are perishing!"

He said to them, "Why, little-faiths, are you fearful?" Then rising he rebuked the winds and the sea, and there was a mega calm.

They marvelled saying, "What sort is this human, whom even the winds and the sea obey?"

RESPONSORY Our hearts fill up with wonder, Lord,
as we contemplate your works.

Let us bless the Lord/.   R. **Thanks be to God/.**

PSALMS of ST. FRANCIS of ASSISI

ADVENT SEASON

Advent Sundays: *Acclamation of the Christ*
7th Psalm of Saint Francis

All you nations, clap your hands!
Shout to God with cries of joy!
Ps 47:2
How awesome is Most High Adonai,
the great Ruler over all the earth.
Ps 47:3
Our Abba of heaven and earth,
our Ruler before all ages,
sent from heaven the Beloved Begotten Son
and brought about salvation
in the center of creation.
Ps 74:12; 144:7; Mt 17:5;
Jn 3:17; Gal 4:4; Creed
Let the heavens rejoice and the earth be glad;
let the sea resound and all its fullness;
let the fields and all that is in them be jubilant.
Ps 96:11-12a
Sing to Adonai a new song!
Sing to Adonai, all the earth!
Ps 96:1
For great is Adonai, greatly being praised,
To be held in awe beyond all so-called "*gods.*"
Ps 96:4
Take up your cross, follow Jesus,
and abide alive in him.
Mt 16:24; cf. Jn 15:10

•

Advent Mondays: *Time of Expectation*
13th Psalm of Saint Francis

Until when, Lord; will you forget me to forever?
Until when will you hide your faces from me?
Psalm 13:2
Until when must I wrestle with my thinking soul
and sorrow in my heart day by day?
Ps 13:3a
Until when will enmity triumph?
Look! Answer, my God Adonai.
Ps 13:3b-4a
Give light to my eyes
lest enmity say, "I overcame that one."
Ps 13:4b-5a
Foes may rejoice when I fall,
but my trust is in your unfailing love.
Ps 13:5b-6a
My heart rejoices in your salvation.
I will sing to Adonai who is good to me.
Ps 13:6bd

•

Advent Tuesdays: *Vision of Fulfillment*
14th Psalm of Saint Francis

I will praise you, Adonai,
Abba and Lord of heaven and earth,
for you have heard me.
Is 12:1; Mt 11:25; Sir 51:1

Surely God is my salvation!
I will trust and will not be afraid.
Ps 25:5b; Is 12:2a

Adonai is my strength and my song
and became for me salvation.
Is 12:2b; Ex 15:2

Your right hand, Adonai,
magnificent in power,
your right hand, Adonai,
shatters enmity.
Ex 15:6

The poor ones will see and be glad;
may your hearts now live, you seekers of God.
Ps 69:33ab

For Adonai hears the needy ones
and despises not the captives.
Ps 69:34

Let heaven and earth give praise
with the seas and all moving in them.
Ps 69:35

For God will save Zion
and rebuild the cities of Judah.
Ps 69:36ab

Then they will settle there
and be her steward.
Ps 69:36c

The children of the servants will inherit her
and lovers of the Name will dwell in her.
Ps 69:37

•

Advent Wednesdays: *Shout of Joy*
10th Psalm of Saint Francis

Shout joy to God all you earth!
Sing the glory of the name!
Offer glory and praise to God!
Ps 66:1-2

Say to God, "How awesome are you;
how great are your deeds."
Enmity cringes before you and your power.
Ps 66:3

All of the earth bow down to you,
they sing praise to you,
they sing praise to your name.
Ps 66:4

Come! Listen! Let me tell all who fear God
what God has done for my very self.
Ps 66:16

To God my mouth cried out
with praise on my tongue.
Ps 66:17

I cried for help from my God,
who heard from the temple my voice;
my cry went into these ears.
Ps 18:7cd

Peoples, make heard
the praise of our God!
Ps 66:8

May the name endure to forever
and continue as long as the sun;
being thus blessed, may the nations bless.
Ps 72:17cd

Blessed be God Adonai, God of Israel,
alone doing marvelous deeds.
Ps 72:18; 136:4

Blessed be the glory of the name to forever;
may the earth be filled with the glory of God.
Ps 72:19

•

Advent Thursdays: *Cry of Hope*
11th Psalm of Saint Francis

May Adonai answer you on the day of distress.
May the name of the God of Jacob protect you.
Ps 20:2

May God help you from the sanctuary
and support you from Zion.
Ps 20:3

May God remember all your burnt offerings
and accept all of your sacrifices.
Ps 20:4

May God give to you as your heart desires
and make all of your plans succeed.
Ps 20:5

We will shout for joy at your victory
and lift a banner in the name of our God.
Ps 20:6

Advent
Thursdays, continued

May the Lord grant all your requests.
Ps 20:7ab

Now I know that Adonai sends
the chosen anointed, Jesus Christ the Son,
to judge peoples with justice.
Ps 20:7cd; 9:9b; Jn 3:17

Adonai is the refuge for the oppressed,
the stronghold in times of trouble.
May those who know the Name trust in the Lord.
Ps 9:10-11a

Praised be Adonai, my Rock,
my love and fortress, my strong deliverer,
my shield in whom I take refuge.
Ps 144:1b; 59:17cd

To you, my Strength, I sing praise
for you God, my fortress,
you God are my love.
Ps 59:18

•

Advent Fridays: *Prayer of a Child*
12th Psalm of Saint Francis

In you, Adonai, I take refuge;
to forever, let me not be shamed.
In your justice you rescue and deliver me.
Ps 71:1b-2a

Turn your ear to me and save me!
Command that I may be saved.
Ps 71:2b,3b

Be to me as a rock,
and a refuge to go to always.
Ps 71:3a

For you are my hope, Lord Adonai,
my confidence since my youth.
Ps 71:5

I have relied on you from birth;
my praise is ever to you.
Ps 71:6

May my mouth be filled all the day
with praise of your splendor.
Ps 71:8

Answer me, Adonai, for good is your love!
In your great mercies, turn to me!
Ps 69:17

Hide not your faces from your servant;
to my trouble, be quick! Answer me!
Ps 69:18

Praised be Adonai, my Rock,
my love and fortress, my strong deliverer,
my shield in whom I take refuge.
Ps 144:1b; 59:17cd

To you, my Strength, I sing praise
for you God, my fortress,
you God are my love.
Ps 59:18

•

Advent Saturdays: *Morning Sun*
3rd Psalm of Saint Francis

Have mercy on me, God, have mercy on me,
for in you my soul takes refuge.
Ps 57:2a

In the shade of your wings I take refuge
until disasters pass.
Ps 57:2b

I cry out to God Most High,
to God who fulfills me.
Ps 57:3

God sends from the heavens and saves me
and rebukes the one pursuing me.
Ps 57:4ab

God sends love and fidelity
and rescues me from enmity,
from those too strong for me.
Ps 57:4c-5a; 18:18

For my feet they spread a net
and my self was bowed down.
Ps 57:ab

Before me they dug a pit
and fell into it themselves.
Ps 57:cd

My heart is steadfast, God,
my heart is steadfast;
I will sing and make music.
Ps 57:8

Awake, my glory,
wake up the harp and the lyre;
I will wake up the dawn.
Ps 57:9

I will praise you among the nations, Lord;
I will sing of you among the peoples.
Ps 57:10

For great to the heavens is your love
and to the skies is your fidelity.
Ps 57:11

Be exalted above the heavens, God,
your glory over all the earth.
Ps 57:12

•

CHRISTMAS SEASON

Christmas Sundays, Mondays, Wednesdays, & Fridays:
Origin and Birth of Christ
15th Psalm of Saint Francis

Sing for joy to God our strength;
turn to God, the living and true.
Shout to God with cries of joy!
Ps 81:2a; 1 Th 1:9; Ps 47:2

How awesome is Most High Adonai,
the great Ruler over all the earth.
Ps 47:3

Christmas
Sundays, Mondays, Wednesdays & Fridays, continued

Our Abba of heaven and earth,
the Ruler before all the ages,
sent from heaven the Beloved Begotten Son
to be born of the Blessed Virgin Mary.
Ps 74:12a; 144:7; Ga 4:4; Creed

The Son called out: "you are my Abba,"
who appointed him as the firstborn
and most exalted above rulers of the earth.
Ps 89:27a,28

By day Adonai directs Merciful Love
and at night the song within us.
Ps 42:9ab

This is the day Adonai has made;
let us rejoice and be glad in it.
Ps 118:24

A child is born to us, a Son is given to us,
born to us on the way and laid in a manger
because there was no place in the inn.
Is 9:5; Lk 2:7,12,16

Glory to God on high
and on earth peace to people of good will.
Lk 2:14

Let the heavens rejoice and the earth be glad;
let the sea resound and all its fullness;
let the fields and all that is in them be jubilant.
Ps 96:11-12a

Sing to Adonai a new song!
Sing to Adonai, all the earth!
Ps 96:1

For great is Adonai, greatly being praised,
to be held in awe above all so-called "gods."
Ps 96:4

Ascribe to Adonai, families of nations!
Acknowledge Adonai as glory and strength!
Give to Adonai the glory of the Name!
Ps 96:7-8a

•

Christmas Tuesdays & Saturdays:
Morning Sun
3rd Psalm of Saint Francis

Have mercy on me, God, have mercy on me,
for in you my soul takes refuge.
Ps 57:2a

In the shade of your wings I take refuge
until disasters pass.
Ps 57:2b

I cry out to God Most High,
to God who fulfills me.
Ps 57:3

God sends from the heavens and saves me
and rebukes the one pursuing me.
Ps 57:4ab

God sends love and fidelity
and rescues me from enmity,
from those too strong for me.
Ps 57:4c-5a; 18:18

Christmas
Tuesdays & Saturdays, continued

For my feet they spread a net
and my self was bowed down.
Ps 57:ab

Before me they dug a pit
and fell into it themselves.
Ps 57:cd

My heart is steadfast, God,
my heart is steadfast;
I will sing and make music.
Ps 57:8

Awake, my glory,
wake up the harp and the lyre;
I will wake up the dawn.
Ps 57:9

I will praise you among the nations, Lord;
I will sing of you among the peoples.
Ps 57:10

For great to the heavens is your love
and to the skies is your fidelity.
Ps 57:11

Be exalted above the heavens, God,
your glory over all the earth.
Ps 57:12

●

Christmas Thursdays:
Echoes of Struggle & Victory
8th Psalm of Saint Francis

O God, come to save me;
Adonai, make haste to help me.
Ps 70:2

May plans to seek my life
be shamed and confused.
Ps 70:3a

May the desire for my ruin
be turned back in disgrace.
Ps 70:3b

May the ones saying, "aha!, aha!"
turn back in shame.
Ps 70:4

May all who seek you
rejoice in you and be glad.
Ps 70:5a

May lovers of salvation say always,
"Let God be exalted."
Ps 70:5b

Yet I am poor and needy, God;
come quickly.
Ps 70:6a

Adonai, my help and deliverer,
do not delay.
Ps 70:6b

●

LENTEN SEASON

Lent Sundays: *Acclamation of the Christ*
7th Psalm of Saint Francis

All you nations, clap your hands!
Shout to God with cries of joy!
Ps 47:2
How awesome is Most High Adonai,
the great Ruler over all the earth.
Ps 47:3
Our Abba of heaven and earth,
our Ruler before all ages,
sent from heaven the Beloved Begotten Son
and brought about salvation
in the center of creation.
Ps 74:12; 144:7; Mt 17:5;
Jn 3:17; Gal 4:4; Creed
Let the heavens rejoice and the earth be glad;
let the sea resound and all its fullness;
let the fields and all that is in them be jubilant.
Ps 96:11-12a
Sing to Adonai a new song!
Sing to Adonai, all the earth!
Ps 96:1
For great is Adonai, greatly being praised,
To be held in awe beyond all so-called "*gods*."
Ps 96:4

Take up your cross, follow Jesus,
and abide alive in him.
Mt 16:24; cf. Jn 15:10

Worship Adonai in holy splendor!
Tremble in the presence all you earth!
Say among the nations, "Adonai reigns!"
Ps 96:9b-10a

He ascended into heaven and is seated
at the right hand of God the Father almighty.
Apostles' Creed

Be exalted, God, above the heavens,
your glory over all the earth.
Ps 57:12

We know that the Son of God comes
and will come to judge with justice.
1 Jn 5:20; Ps 96:13b; 75:3

●

Lent Mondays: *Gethsemane*
1st Psalm of Saint Francis

O God, my laments are in your record
and my tears are in your wineskin.
Ps 56:9

Together against me they whisper,
imagining the worst for me,
waiting on my life, conspiring together.
Ps 41:8a; 71:10c

Lent
Mondays, continued

They repay good with the bad
and hatred for my friendship.
Ps 109:5

In return for my friendship they slander me,
though I pray for them.
Ps 109:4ab

Be not far from me, holy Abba,
ruler of heaven and earth,
for trouble is near with no one to help.
Mt 26:42; Jn 17:11; Ps 22:12

Enmity will turn back on the day I call;
I will know that God is for me.
Ps 56:10

My friends and companions from the past
avoid being present to my woundedness,
and my neighbors stay far away.
Ps 38:12

Holy Abba, be not far away;
come quickly to help me, my Strength!
Jn 17:11; Ps 22:20

Come quickly to help,
my Lord, my salvation.
Ps 38:23

●

Lent Tuesdays: *The Sanhedrin*
2nd Psalm of Saint Francis

God Adonai, my Savior,
I cry out day and night before you.
Ps 88:2

May my prayer come before you;
turn your ear to my cry.
Ps 88:3

Come near because of the adversity;
rescue my soul and redeem me!
Ps 69:19; 30:2

You brought me out from the womb,
to trust in you at the breasts of my mother.
From the womb I was cast upon you.
Ps 22:10-11a

From my very birth, you are my God;
be not far from me.
Ps 22:11b-12

You know my scorn and shame and disgrace,
and you know my reverence.
Ps 69:20a

Enmity stands before you;
scorn broke my heart and I became helpless.
Ps 69:20b-21a

I looked for compassion but there was none,
and for comforters, but found none.
Ps 69:21b-d

Lent
Tuesdays, continued

Arrogant ones attack against me, God;
a band of ruthless people seek my life
and they do not see you before them.
Ps 86:14

I am counted among those going down the pit,
like a human without strength,
set apart with the dead ones.
Ps 88:5-6a

You are my Holy Abba,
my Ruler and my God.
Ps 89:27; 44:5a

Come quickly to help,
my Lord, my salvation.
Ps 38:23

•

Lent Wednesdays: *Morning Sun*
3rd Psalm of Saint Francis

Have mercy on me, God, have mercy on me,
for in you my soul takes refuge.
Ps 57:2a

In the shade of your wings I take refuge
until disasters pass.
Ps 57:2b

I cry out to God Most High,
to God who fulfills me.
Ps 57:3

God sends from the heavens and saves me
and rebukes the one pursuing me.
Ps 57:4ab

God sends love and fidelity
and rescues me from enmity,
from those too strong for me.
Ps 57:4c-5a; 18:18

For my feet they spread a net
and my self was bowed down.
Ps 57:ab

Before me they dug a pit
and fell into it themselves.
Ps 57:cd

My heart is steadfast, God,
my heart is steadfast;
I will sing and make music.
Ps 57:8

Awake, my glory, wake up the harp and the lyre;
I will wake up the dawn.
Ps 57:9

I will praise you among the nations, Lord;
I will sing of you among the peoples.
Ps 57:10

For great to the heavens is your love
and to the skies is your fidelity.
Ps 57:11

Be exalted above the heavens, God,
your glory over all the earth.
Ps 57:12

●

Lent Thursdays: *Pontius Pilate*
4th Psalm of Saint Francis

Be merciful to me, my God!
Human beings pursue me all the day,
attacking with oppression and with slander.
Ps 56:2

Indeed in their pride
do the many attack me.
Ps 56:3

Enmity asks in malice,
"When will that one die and be forgotten?"
When they come to see me
they speak with false hearts to gather slander.
Ps 41:8b-9a

Enmity speaks against me,
waiting on my life, conspiring together.
Ps 71:10b

They go out to the outside to speak;
together against me they whisper.
Ps 41:7

All those seeing me mock at me;
they shake their heads in insult.
Ps 22:8

I am as a worm and a no-human,
the scorn of humanity and despised by people.
Ps 22:7

The utter contempt of even my neighbors,
I am a dread to my friends
who see me on the street and flee.
Ps 31:12ab

Holy Abba, be not far away;
come quickly to help me, my Strength!
Jn 17:11; Ps 22:20

Come quickly to help,
my Lord, my salvation.
Ps 38:23

•

Lent Fridays: *The Cross*
5th *Psalm of Saint Francis*

My voice asks for mercy,
my voice cries to Adonai.
Ps 142:2

Before whom I pour out my complaint,
before whom I tell my trouble.
Ps 142:3

When my spirit grows faint within me
then you know my way.
Ps 142:4ab

In the path where I walk
they hid a snare for me.
Ps 142:4cd

Look right and see:
the one with concern for me
has fled away from me for refuge.
Ps 142:5ab

There is no one who cares for my life.
Ps 142:5cd

For your sake I endure scorn
and shame covers my face.
Ps 69:8

I am a stranger to my brothers and sisters,
an alien to the children of my mother.
Ps 69:9

Holy Abba, zeal for you house consumes me
and insults of your insulters fall on me.
Jn 17:11; Ps 69:10

At my stumbling they took glee
and gathered and gathered attackers
and did not cease to slander.
Ps 35:15

Those hating me for no reason
are more numerous than the hairs of my head.
Ps 69:5ab

Many are the ones destroying me
in enmity and for no reason.
What I did not steal, must I now restore?
Ps 69:5cd

Ruthless witnesses come forward;
on things I do not know they question me.
Ps 35:11

They repay me bad for the good;
when I seek the good they slander me.
Ps 35:12a; 38:21

You are my Holy Abba,
my Ruler and my God.
Ps 44:5

Come quickly to help,
my Lord, my salvation.
Ps 38:23

•

Lent Saturdays: *Death on the Cross*
6th Psalm of Saint Francis

All of you passing by the way, consider and see
if there is a sorrow like my sorrow.
Lam 1:12ab

Dogs indeed surround around me,
a band of doers of the bad encircles me as a lion.
Ps 22:17

They stare and they gloat over me;
they divide my garments among them
and for my clothing they cast lots.
Ps 22:18b,19

They make ready
to tear into my hands and my feet;
I can count all of my bones.
Ps 22:17c-18a

They open wide their mouths against me,
lions tearing up prey and roaring.
Ps 22:14

Like the waters I am poured out
and my bones are all out of joint.
Ps 22:15ab

My heart like wax
melts away within my insides.
Ps 22:15c

Like a broken clay pot, my strength is dried up;
my tongue is stuck in the roof of my mouth.
Ps 22:16ab

They put gall in my food
and for my thirst gave me vinegar to drink.
Ps 69:22

They lay me in the dust of death;
I am in pain and suffering.
Ps 22:16c; 69:27b

I lie down and sleep, and wake up again;
my Abba will take me after the glory.
Ps 3:6; 73:24c

Holy Abba, you hold me by my right hand
and guide me with your counsel
and will take me after the glory.
Jn 17:11; Ps 73:24

Who in the heavens is for me?
With you, nothing on earth do I desire.
Ps 73:25

Behold, behold, for I am God, says Adonai.
I will be exalted among the nations;
I will be exalted on the earth.
see Ps 2:7; Ps 46:11b

Blessed be Adonai, God of Israel,
who redeems the servants of the Lord
and will not abandon any who take this refuge.
Lk 1:68a; Ps 72:18a;
Ps 34:23a; Heb 9:12

We know that the Son of God comes
and will come to judge with justice.
1 Jn 5:20; Ps 96:13b; 75:3

•

EASTER SEASON

Easter Sundays & Wednesdays:
The New Song
9th Psalm of Saint Francis

Sing to Adonai a new song
who has done marvelous things,
Ps 98:1ab

Working salvation through the Beloved Son,
at the right hand and holy arm.
Ps 98:1cd

Adonai has made known salvation,
justice revealed for the eyes of the nations.
Ps 98:2

By day Adonai directs Merciful Love
and at night the song within us.
Ps 42:9ab

This is the day Adonai has made;
let us rejoice and be glad in it.
Ps 118:24

Blessed is the one coming in the name of Adonai;
our God Adonai has shined light onto us.
Ps 118:26a,27a

Let the heavens rejoice and the earth be glad.
Let the sea resound and all its fullness.
Let the fields and all that is in them be jubilant.
Ps 96:11-12a

Ascribe to Adonai, families of nations!
Acknowledge Adonai as glory and strength!
Give to Adonai the glory of the Name!
Ps 96:7-8a

PSALMS of ST FRANCIS of ASSISI

From Ascension to Pentecost, add:

Peoples of the earth, sing to God!
Sing praise to the Lord!
Ps 68:33a

Rider in the skies, the ancient heavens, see!
The voice thunders, the voice of might.
Ps 68:33b-34a

Proclaim the power of God over Israel,
the majesty and power in the skies.
Ps 68:34b-35

Awesome are you, God, in your sanctuary;
the God of Israel gives power and strengths
to the people praising God.
Ps 68:36

•

Easter Mondays & Thursdays:
Acclamation of the Christ
7th Psalm of Saint Francis

All you nations, clap your hands!
Shout to God with cries of joy!
Ps 47:2
How awesome is Most High Adonai,
the great Ruler over all the earth.
Ps 47:3
Our Abba of heaven and earth,
our Ruler before all ages,
sent from heaven the Beloved Begotten Son
and brought about salvation
in the center of creation.
Ps 74:12; 144:7; Mt 17:5;
Jn 3:17; Gal 4:4; Creed
Let the heavens rejoice and the earth be glad;
let the sea resound and all its fullness;
let the fields and all that is in them be jubilant.
Ps 96:11-12a
Sing to Adonai a new song!
Sing to Adonai, all the earth!
Ps 96:1
For great is Adonai, greatly being praised,
To be held in awe beyond all so-called "*gods*."
Ps 96:4
Take up your cross, follow Jesus,
and abide alive in him.
Mt 16:24; cf. Jn 15:10

Worship Adonai in holy splendor!
Tremble in the presence all you earth!
Say among the nations, "Adonai reigns!"
Ps 96:9b-10a

He ascended into heaven and is seated
at the right hand of God the Father almighty.
Apostles' Creed

Be exalted, God, above the heavens,
your glory over all the earth.
Ps 57:12

We know that the Son of God comes
and will come to judge with justice.
1 Jn 5:20; Ps 96:13b; 75:3

•

Easter Tuesdays & Fridays:
Echoes of Struggle & Victory
8th Psalm of Saint Francis

O God, come to save me;
Adonai, make haste to help me.
Ps 70:2

May plans to seek my life
be shamed and confused.
Ps 70:3a

May the desire for my ruin
be turned back in disgrace.
Ps 70:3b

Easter Tuesdays & Fridays, continued

May the ones saying, "aha!, aha!"
turn back in shame.
Ps 70:4

May all who seek you
rejoice in you and be glad.
Ps 70:5a

May lovers of salvation say always,
"Let God be exalted."
Ps 70:5b

Yet I am poor and needy, God;
come quickly.
Ps 70:6a

Adonai, my help and deliverer,
do not delay.
Ps 70:6b

•

Easter Saturdays:
Morning Sun
3rd *Psalm of Saint Francis*

Have mercy on me, God, have mercy on me,
for in you my soul takes refuge.
Ps 57:2a

In the shade of your wings I take refuge
until disasters pass.
Ps 57:2b

I cry out to God Most High,
to God who fulfills me.
Ps 57:3

God sends from the heavens and saves me
and rebukes the one pursuing me.
Ps 57:4ab

God sends love and fidelity
and rescues me from enmity,
from those too strong for me.
Ps 57:4c-5a; 18:18

For my feet they spread a net
and my self was bowed down.
Ps 57:ab

Before me they dug a pit
and fell into it themselves.
Ps 57:cd

My heart is steadfast, God,
my heart is steadfast;
I will sing and make music.
Ps 57:8

Awake, my glory, wake up the harp and the lyre;
I will wake up the dawn.
Ps 57:9

I will praise you among the nations, Lord;
I will sing of you among the peoples.
Ps 57:10

For great to the heavens is your love
and to the skies is your fidelity.
Ps 57:11

Be exalted above the heavens, God,
your glory over all the earth.
Ps 57:12

•

To PRAY the GOSPEL of the DAY with the CHURCH

ADVENT

The Sunday nearest to November 30:

Sunday - Week 1
- A Matthew 24:37-44
- B Mark 13:33-37
- C Luke 21:25-28,34-36
- Mon Matthew 8:5-11
- Tue Luke 10:21-24
- Wed Matthew 15:29-37
- Thu Matthew 7:21,24-27
- Fri Matthew 9:27-31
- Sat Matthew 9:35-10:1,5a,6-8

Sunday - Week 2
- A Matthew 3:1-12
- B Mark 1:1-8
- C Luke 3:1-6
- Mon Luke 5:17-26
- Tue Matthew 18:12-14
- Wed Matthew 11:28-30
- Thu Matthew 11:11-15
- Fri Matthew 11:16-19
- Sat Matthew 17:9a,10-13

Sunday - Week 3
- A Matthew 11:2-11
- B John 1:6-8,19-28
- C Luke 3:10-18
- Mon Matthew 21:23-27
- Tue Matthew 21:28-32
- Wed Luke 7:18b-23
- Thu Luke 7:24-30
- Fri John 5:33-36

Sunday - Week 4
- A Matthew 1:18-24
- B Luke 1:26-38
- C Luke 1:39-45

- Dec 17 Matthew 1:1-17
- Dec 18 Matthew 1:18-25
- Dec 19 Luke 1:5-25
- Dec 20 Luke 1:26-38
- Dec 21 Luke 1:39-45
- Dec 22 Luke 1:46-56
- Dec 23 Luke 1:57-66
- Dec 24 Luke 1:67-79

CHRISTMAS

December 25 is Christmas Day.
- Vigil Matthew 1:1-25
- Midnight Luke 2:1-14
- Dawn Luke 2:15-20
- Day John 1:1-18

- Dec 26 Mt 10:17-22 Stephen
- Dec 27 John 20:1a,2-8 John
- Dec 28 Mt 2:13-18 Innocents
- Dec 29 Luke 2:22-35
- Dec 30 Luke 2:36-40
- Dec 31 John 1:1-18

Holy Family Sunday
- A Mt 2:13-15,19-23
- B Luke 2:22-40
- C Luke 2:41-52

DAILY GOSPEL READINGS

CHRISTMAS, continued

Mary, Mother of God
Jan 1 Luke 2:16-21

Jan 2 John 1:19-28
Jan 3 John 1:29:34
Jan 4 John 1:35-42
Jan 5 John 1:43-51
Jan 6 Mark 1:7-11
Jan 7 John 2:1-11

Epiphany Sunday (or Jan 6)
ABC Matthew 2:1-12

After Epiphany
Mon Matthew 4:12-17,23-25
Tue Mark 6:34-44
Wed Mark 6:45-52
Thu Luke 4:14-22a
Fri Luke 5:12-16
Sat John 3:22-30

Baptism of the Lord
A Matthew 3:13-17
B Mark 1:7-11
C Luke 3:15-16,21-22

The Feast of the Baptism of the Lord concludes the Season of Christmas. Ordinary Time, Week 1, begins on the following day. See page 159.

LENT

Lent begins with Ash Wednesday, 6 weeks and 4 days prior to Easter. See the table on page 158.

Ash Wed Matt 6:1-6,16-18

Thu Luke 9:22-25
Fri Matthew 9:14-15
Sat Luke 5:27-32

Sunday - Week 1
A Matthew 4:1-11
B Mark 1:12-15
C Luke 4:1-13
Mon Matt 25:31-46
Tue Matthew 6:7-15
Wed Luke 11:29-32
Thu Matthew 7:7-12
Fri Matthew 5:20-26
Sat Matthew 5:43-48

Sunday - Week 2
A Matthew 17:1-9
B Mark 9:2-10
C Luke 9:28b-36
Mon Luke 6:36-38
Tue Matthew 23:1-12
Wed Matt 20:17-28
Thu Luke 16:19-31
Fri Mt 21:33-43,45-46
Sat Lk 15:1-3,11-32

LENT, continued

Sunday – Week 3
- A   John 4:5-42
- B   John 2:13-25
- C   Luke 13:1-9
- Mon   Luke 4:24-30
- Tue   Matthew 18:21-35
- Wed   Matthew 5:17-19
- Thu   Luke 11:14-23
- Fri   Mark 12:28-34
- Sat   Luke 18:9-14

Sunday – Week 4
- A   John 9:1-41
- B   John 3:14-21
- C   Luke 15:1-3,11-32
- Mon   John 4:43-54
- Tue   John 5:1-16
- Wed   John 5:17-30
- Thu   John 5:31-47
- Fri   John 7:1-2,10,25-30
- Sat   John 7:40-53

Sunday – Week 5
- A   John 11:1-45
- B   John 12:20-33
- C   John 8:1-11
- Mon   John 8:12-20
- Tue   John 8:21-30
- Wed   John 8:31-42
- Thu   John 8:51-59
- Fri   John 10:31-42
- Sat   John 11:45-56

HOLY WEEK

Palm Sunday
Year A
Procession   Matt 21:1-11
Passion   Matt 26:14-27:66
Year B
Procession   Mark 11:1-10
Passion   Mark 14:1-15:47
Year C
Procession   Luke 19:28-40
Passion   Luke 22:14-23:56

Holy Week Weekdays
- Mon   John 12:1-11
- Tue   Jn 13:21-33,36-38
- Wed   Matt 26:14-25

Chrism Mass
Cathedral   Luke 4:16-21

Holy Thursday
Evening   John 13:1-15

Good Friday
Passion   John 18:1-19:42

EASTER

Easter Vigil
- A Matthew 28:1-10
- B Mark 16:1-7
- C Luke 24:1-12

*Easter Sunday is
the first Sunday
following the first full moon
following the vernal equinox.*

Octave of Easter
Easter Day
- ABC John 20:1-9
  (or vigil reading)
- Mon Matthew 28:8-15
- Tue John 20:11-18
- Wed Luke 24:13-35
- Thu Luke 24:35-48
- Fri John 21:1-14
- Sat Mark 16:9-15

Second Sunday in
the Octave of Easter
- ABC John 20:19-31

Week 2
- Mon John 3:1-8
- Tue John 3:7b-15
- Wed John 3:16-21
- Thu John 3:31-36
- Fri John 6:1-15
- Sat John 6:16-21

Sunday - Week 3
- A Luke 24:13-35
- B Luke 24:35-48
- C John 21:1-19
- Mon John 6:22-29
- Tue John 6:30-35
- Wed John 6:35-40
- Thu John 6:44-51
- Fri John 6:52-59
- Sat John 6:60-69

Sunday - Week 4
- A John 10:1-10
- B John 10:11-18
- C John 10:27-30
- Mon Jn 10:1-10 or 11-18
- Tue John 10:22-30
- Wed John 12:44-50
- Thu John 13:16-20
- Fri John 14:1-6
- Sat John 14:7-14

Sunday - Week 5
- A John 14:1-12
- B John 15:1-8
- C Jn 13:31-33a,34-35
- Mon John 14:21-26
- Tue John 14:27-31a
- Wed John 15:1-8
- Thu John 15:9-11
- Fri John 15:12-17
- Sat John 15:18-21

EASTER, continued

Sunday - Week 6
- A   John 14:15-21
- B   John 15:9-17
- C   John 14:23-29
- Mon   John 15:26 - 16:4a
- Tue   John 16:5-11
- Wed   John 16:12-15
- Thu   John 16:16-20
- Fri   John 16:20-23
- Sat   John 16:23b-28

Sunday - Ascension
- A   Matthew 28:16-20
- B   Mark 16:15-20
- C   Luke 24:46-53

In some places Ascension is celebrated on Thursday of Week 6.

When Thursday of Week 6 is Ascension:
Sunday - Week 7
- A   John 17:1-11a
- B   John 17:11b-19
- C   John 17:20-26

Week 7
- Mon   John 16:29-33
- Tue   John 17:1-11a
- Wed   John 17:11b-19
- Thu   John 17:20-26
- Fri   John 21:15-19
- Sat   John 21:20-25

PENTECOST
- Vigil   John 7:37-39
- Day   John 20:19-23

YEAR	ASH WEDNESDAY	EASTER	PENTECOST	MONDAY & WEEK ORDINARY TIME RESUMES	
2023 A	Feb. 22	April 9	May 28	May 29	Week 8
2024 B	Feb. 14	March 31	May 19	May 20	Week 7
2025 C	Mar. 5	April 20	June 8	June 9	Week 10
2026 A	Feb. 18	April 5	May 24	May 25	Week 8
2027 B	Feb. 10	Mar 28	May 16	May 17	Week 7
2028 C	Mar. 1	April 16	June 4	June 5	Week 9
2029 A	Feb. 14	April 1	May 20	May 21	Week 7
2030 B	Mar. 6	April 21	June 9	June 10	Week 10
2031 C	Feb. 26	April 12	May 31	June 1	Week 9
2032 A	Feb. 17	April 4	May 23	May 24	Week 8
2033 B	Mar. 9	April 24	June 12	June 13	Week 11
2034 C	Feb. 22	April 9	May 28	May 29	Week 8

DAILY GOSPEL READINGS

ORDINARY TIME

Week 1
Mon	Mark 1:14-20
Tue	Mark 1:21-28
Wed	Mark 1:29-39
Thu	Mark 1:40-45
Fri	Mark 2:1-12
Sat	Mark 2:13-17

Ordinary Time begins after the Christmas Feast of the Baptism of the Lord. Ordinary Time breaks for the seasons of Lent and Easter.

Ordinary Time resumes on the Monday following Pentecost Sunday.

Holy Trinity Sunday
(Sunday after Pentecost)
- A John 3:16-18
- B Matthew 28:16-20
- C John 16:12-15

Body and Blood
(Sunday after Trinity Sunday)
- A John 6:51-58
- B Mark 14:12-16,22-26
- C Luke 9:11b-17

Sacred Heart
(Friday after Body and Blood)
- A Matthew 11:25-30
- B John 19:31-37
- C Luke 15:3-7

Sunday - Week 2
A	John 1:29-34
B	John 1:35-42
C	John 2:1-11
Mon	Mark 2:18-22
Tue	Mark 2:23-28
Wed	Mark 3:1-6
Thu	Mark 3:7-12
Fri	Mark 3:13-19
Sat	Mark 3:20-21

Sunday - Week 3
A	Matthew 4:12-23
B	Mark 1:14-20
C	Lk 1:1-4; 4:14-21
Mon	Mark 3:22-30
Tue	Mark 3:31-35
Wed	Mark 4:1-20
Thu	Mark 4:21-25
Fri	Mark 4:26-34
Sat	Mark 4:35-41

Sunday - Week 4
A	Matthew 5:1-12a
B	Mark 1:21-28
C	Luke 4:21-30
Mon	Mark 5:1-20
Tue	Mark 5:21-30
Wed	Mark 6:1-6
Thu	Mark 6:7-13
Fri	Mark 6:14-29
Sat	Mark 6:30-34

ORDINARY TIME, continued

Sunday - Week 5
- A   Matthew 5:13-16
- B   Mark 1:29-39
- C   Luke 5:1-11
- Mon   Mark 6:53-56
- Tue   Mark 7:1-13
- Wed   Mark 7:14-23
- Thu   Mark 7:24-30
- Fri   Mark 7:31-37
- Sat   Mark 8:1-10

Sunday - Week 6
- A   Matthew 5:17-37
- B   Mark 1:40-45
- C   Luke 6:17,20-26
- Mon   Mark 8:11-13
- Tue   Mark 8:14-21
- Wed   Mark 8:22-26
- Thu   Mark 8:27-33
- Fri   Mark 8:34 - 9:1
- Sat   Mark 9:2-13

Sunday - Week 7
- A   Matthew 5:38-48
- B   Mark 2:1-12
- C   Luke 6:27-38
- Mon   Mark 9:14-29
- Tue   Mark 9:30-37
- Wed   Mark 9:38-40
- Thu   Mark 9:41-50
- Fri   Mark 10:1-12
- Sat   Mark 10:13-16

Sunday - Week 8
- A   Matthew 6:24-34
- B   Mark 2:18-22
- C   Luke 6:39-45
- Mon   Mark 10:17-27
- Tue   Mark 10:28-31
- Wed   Mark 10:32-45
- Thu   Mark 10:46-52
- Fri   Mark 11:11-26
- Sat   Mark 11:27-33

Sunday - Week 9
- A   Matthew 7:21-27
- B   Mark 2:23 - 3:6
- C   Luke 7:1-10
- Mon   Mark 12:1-12
- Tue   Mark 12:13-17
- Wed   Mark 12:18-27
- Thu   Mark 12:28-34
- Fri   Mark 12:35-37
- Sat   Mark 12:38-44

Sunday - Week 10
- A   Matthew 9:9-13
- B   Mark 3:20-35
- C   Luke 7:11-17
- Mon   Matthew 5:1-12
- Tue   Matthew 5:13-16
- Wed   Matthew 5:17-19
- Thu   Matthew 5:20-26
- Fri   Matthew 5:27-32
- Sat   Matthew 5:33-37

DAILY GOSPEL READINGS

ORDINARY TIME, continued

Sunday - Week 11
- A Matthew 9:36 - 10:8
- B Mark 4:26-34
- C Luke 7:36 - 8:3
- Mon Matthew 5:38-42
- Tue Matthew 5:43-48
- Wed Matthew 6:1-6,16-18
- Thu Matthew 6:7-15
- Fri Matthew 6:19-23
- Sat Matthew 6:24-34

Sunday - Week 12
- A Matthew 10:26-33
- B Mark 4:35-41
- C Luke 9:18-24
- Mon Matthew 7:1-5
- Tue Matthew 7:6,12-14
- Wed Matthew 7:15-20
- Thu Matthew 7:21-29
- Fri Matthew 8:1-4
- Sat Matthew 8:5-17

Sunday - Week 13
- A Matthew 10:37-42
- B Mark 5:21-43
- C Luke 9:51-62
- Mon Matthew 8:18-22
- Tue Matthew 8:23-27
- Wed Matthew 8:28-34
- Thu Matthew 9:1-8
- Fri Matthew 9:9-13
- Sat Matthew 9:14-17

Sunday - Week 14
- A Matthew 11:25-30
- B Mark 6:1-6
- C Luke 10:1-12,17-20
- Mon Matthew 9:18-26
- Tue Matthew 9:32-38
- Wed Matthew 10:1-7
- Thu Matthew 10:7-15
- Fri Matthew 10:16-23
- Sat Matthew 10:24-33

Sunday - Week 15
- A Matthew 13:1-23
- B Mark 6:7-13
- C Luke 10:25-37
- Mon Matt 10:34 - 11:1
- Tue Matthew 11:20-24
- Wed Matthew 11:25-27
- Thu Matthew 11:28-30
- Fri Matthew 12:1-8
- Sat Matthew 12:14-21

Sunday - Week 16
- A Matthew 13:24-43
- B Mark 6:30-34
- C Luke 10:38-42
- Mon Matthew 12:38-42
- Tue Matthew 12:46-50
- Wed Matthew 13:1-9
- Thu Matthew 13:10-17
- Fri Matthew 13:18-23
- Sat Matthew 13:24-30

ORDINARY TIME, continued

Sunday - Week 17
- A Matthew 13:44-52
- B John 6:1-15
- C Luke 11:1-13
- Mon Matthew 13:31-35
- Tue Matthew 13:36-43
- Wed Matthew 13:44-46
- Thu Matthew 13:47-53
- Fri Matthew 13:54-58
- Sat Matthew 14:1-12

Sunday - Week 18
- A Matthew 14:13-21
- B John 6:24-35
- C Luke 12:13-21
- Mon Matthew 14:22-36
- Tue Matthew 15:1-2,10-14
- Wed Matthew 15:21-28
- Thu Matthew 16:13-23
- Fri Matthew 16:24-28
- Sat Matthew 17:14-20

Sunday - Week 19
- A Matthew 14:22-33
- B John 6:41-51
- C Luke 12:32-48
- Mon Matthew 17:22-27
- Tue Matthew 18:1-5,10,12-14
- Wed Matthew 18:15-20
- Thu Matthew 18:21 - 19:1
- Fri Matthew 19:3-12
- Sat Matthew 19:13-15

Sunday - Week 20
- A Matthew 15:21-28
- B John 6:51-58
- C Luke 12:49-53
- Mon Matthew 19:16-22
- Tue Matthew 19:23-30
- Wed Matthew 20:1-16
- Thu Matthew 22:1-14
- Fri Matthew 22:34-40
- Sat Matthew 23:1-12

Sunday - Week 21
- A Matthew 16:13-20
- B John 6:60-69
- C Luke 13:22-30
- Mon Matthew 23:13-22
- Tue Matthew 23:23-26
- Wed Matthew 23:27-32
- Thu Matthew 24:42-51
- Fri Matthew 25:1-13
- Sat Matthew 25:14-30

Sunday - Week 22
- A Matthew 16:21-27
- B Mk 7:1-8,14-15,21-23
- C Luke 14:1,7-14
- Mon Luke 4:16-30
- Tue Luke 4:31-37
- Wed Luke 4:38-44
- Thu Luke 5:1-11
- Fri Luke 5:33-39
- Sat Luke 6:1-5

DAILY GOSPEL READINGS

ORDINARY TIME, continued

Sunday - Week 23
- A Matthew 18:15-20
- B Mark 7:31-37
- C Luke 14:25-33
- Mon Luke 6:6-11
- Tue Luke 6:12-19
- Wed Luke 6:20-26
- Thu Luke 6:27-38
- Fri Luke 6:39-42
- Sat Luke 6:43-49

Sunday - Week 24
- A Matthew 18:21-35
- B Mark 8:27-35
- C Luke 15:1-32
- Mon Luke 7:1-10
- Tue Luke 7:11-17
- Wed Luke 7:31-35
- Thu Luke 7:36-50
- Fri Luke 8:1-3
- Sat Luke 8:4-15

Sunday - Week 25
- A Matthew 20:1-16a
- B Mark 9:30-37
- C Luke 16:1-13
- Mon Luke 8:16-18
- Tue Luke 8:19-21
- Wed Luke 9:1-6
- Thu Luke 9:7-9
- Fri Luke 9:18-22
- Sat Luke 9:43b-45

Sunday - Week 26
- A Matt 21:28-32
- B Mk 9:38-43,45,47-48
- C Luke 16:19-31
- Mon Luke 9:46-50
- Tue Luke 9:51-56
- Wed Luke 9:57-62
- Thu Luke 10:1-12
- Fri Luke 10:13-16
- Sat Luke 10:17-24

Sunday - Week 27
- A Matt 21:33-43
- B Mark 10:2-16
- C Luke 17:5-10
- Mon Luke 10:25-37
- Tue Luke 10:38-42
- Wed Luke 11:1-4
- Thu Luke 11:5-13
- Fri Luke 11:15-26
- Sat Luke 11:27-28

Sunday - Week 28
- A Matthew 22:1-14
- B Mark 10:17-30
- C Luke 17:11-19
- Mon Luke 11:29-32
- Tue Luke 11:37-41
- Wed Luke 11:42-46
- Thu Luke 11:47-54
- Fri Luke 12:1-7
- Sat Luke 12:8-12

ORDINARY TIME, continued

Sunday - Week 29
- A   Matthew 22:15-21
- B   Mark 10:35-45
- C   Luke 18:1-8
- Mon   Luke 12:13-21
- Tue   Luke 12:35-38
- Wed   Luke 12:39-48
- Thu   Luke 12:49-53
- Fri   Luke 12:54-59
- Sat   Luke 13:1-9

Sunday - Week 30
- A   Matthew 22:34-40
- B   Mark 10:46-52
- C   Luke 18:9-14
- Mon   Luke 13:10-17
- Tue   Luke 13:18-21
- Wed   Luke 13:22-30
- Thu   Luke 13:31-35
- Fri   Luke 14:1-6
- Sat   Luke 14:1,7-11

Sunday - Week 31
- A   Matthew 23:1-12
- B   Mark 12:28b-34
- C   Luke 19:1-10
- Mon   Luke 14:12-14
- Tue   Luke 14:15-24
- Wed   Luke 14:25-33
- Thu   Luke 15:1-10
- Fri   Luke 16:1-8
- Sat   Luke 16:9-15

Sunday - Week 32
- A   Matthew 25:1-13
- B   Mark 12:38-44
- C   Luke 20:27-38
- Mon   Luke 17:1-6
- Tue   Luke 17:7-10
- Wed   Luke 17:11-19
- Thu   Luke 17:20-25
- Fri   Luke 17:26-37
- Sat   Luke 18:1-8

Sunday - Week 33
- A   Matt 25:14-30
- B   Mark 13:24-43
- C   Luke 21:5-19
- Mon   Luke 18:35-43
- Tue   Luke 19:1-10
- Wed   Luke 19:11-28
- Thu   Luke 19:41-44
- Fri   Luke 19:45-48
- Sat   Luke 20:27-40

Feast of Christ the King
- A   Matt 25:31-46
- B   John 18:33b-37
- C   Luke 23:35-43

Week 34
- Mon   Luke 21:1-4
- Tue   Luke 21:5-11
- Wed   Luke 21:12-19
- Thu   Luke 21:20-28
- Fri   Luke 21:29-33
- Sat   Luke 21:34-36

LECTIO DIVINA
lek'-see-oh div-ee'-nuh

1. *Lectio* – Read the passage of the word of God with attention, silently, aloud, or in a whisper. If drawn to a word or phrase or image, stop.

2. *Meditatio* – Breathe. Repeat the word or phrase or image over and over as you breathe. Let it sink into your mind, heart, soul and strength. Savor the word. Ask just one question: *Why this? What do you wish to say, Lord?*

3. *Oratio* – Be not afraid to enter into a spontaneous and loving dialogue with God. Talk to God as you would talk to your closest most intimate friend. Be totally honest about what you are thinking and feeling. Are any memories provoked? What do you want to say to God who loves you just the way you are? You may be drawn to praise, thanksgiving, contrition, petition, desires, decisions, resolutions, commitments, dedications... God is interested in everything you have to say and will not judge you. You get to decide whether you will integrate this Word of God into your heart, life and work, or whether you will reject it or dismiss it as of no worth or value to you.

4. *Contemplatio* – For the remainder of the time you have set aside, go back to the word, phrase or image. Breathe. Relax. Simply repeat the word, phrase or image over and over. When distracting thoughts or feelings enter your mind (they will), go back to your word. There is nothing to accomplish; just give this time to the God who loves you. Sitting in God's presence in this silence, you are making an act of faith that God is working in you in God's own time and way. When your time is up, offer a prayer of gratitude. Many people who do *Lectio Divina* find regular journaling helpful.

ACKNOWLEDGEMENTS, SOURCES & CHOICES MADE in this MEDITATION RENDERING

The official translation approved by the Catholic Church for the *Liturgy of the Hours* is a beautiful translation for chanting in monasteries. As a former parish priest for twenty-two years and now in retirement, almost all of my time with the Psalter is with the church universal but alone with God, whether in my room, in a chapel, or in the woods. Praying in *Lectio Divina,* trying to listen to the Lord, I have found much prayerful fruit in several translations.

This meditation rendering follows consciously these choices:

1. For the name *YHVH,* or *Yahweh,* the Hebrew word **Adonai** (ah-duh-nigh') meaning *My Lord,* is used. In several places the words *El* or *Elyon* or *Elohim* are retrieved, as is *Sabaoth* instead of *Mighty* or *Hosts.*

2. Following the Christian understanding of one God in the three persons of the Trinity, masculine pronouns for God are avoided (I really don't know why women tolerate them), except when God is referred to as Father, or specific references to Jesus. I do this as an openly gay cis-gender male.

3. Except in the traditional Lord's Prayer and doxology, rather than the Greek **Father** (*pater*) the more intimate Aramaic *Abba* is used (think Dad, Daddy, Papa) as in Mark 14:36. Among my family and friends, no one addresses their Daddy as Father. See also Saint Paul's use of *Abba* in Romans 8:15 and Galatians 4:6 (see pgs 23, 104).

4. In an admittedly imperfect effort to pray the gospel as well as the psalms, the word *enemy* is most often rendered as *enmity* and *foes* as *adversity.*

5. Where people are referred to as *evil,* the emphasis is shifted to those who *do* the bad, or *ways* that are bad.

6. Since *race* is a human construct, and we are all members of the one human race, words such as *tribe* and *family* are used.

There are problems with all of these choices. Still, in my judgment, the benefits overwhelm the problems.

CHOICES & ACKNOWLEDGEMENTS

Any errors in this rendering are entirely my own. Let us be grateful for all those who do the real work of translating sacred scripture.

The traditional doxology (Father, Son, and Holy Spirit) is from the Matthew 28:19 baptism instructions. These may also be helpful in private prayer; if not, ignore them:

Sundays – Apostles	Father, Son, and Holy Spirit…
Monday – Martyrs	Ruler, Prophet, and Ruah…
Tuesdays – Holy Women	Rock, Physician, and Consoler…
Weds – Pastors/Doctors	All Knowing, Teacher, and Guide…
Thursdays – Holy Men	Almighty, Savior, and Advocate…
Fridays – Virgins	Intimate Friend, Brother, and Sister…
Saturdays – Mary	Creator, Redeemer, and Holy Breath…

SOURCES

The primary source for this work is the grace of three decades with the psalms, canticles and readings from many translations, including:

The Liturgy of the Hours (Four Volumes), Copyright © 1974 ICEL International Committee on English in the Liturgy, Inc.

New American Bible with Revised New Testament, (1986) **and Revised Psalms** (1991) Copyright © 1991, 1986, 1970 Confraternity of Christian Doctrine, Inc. Washington, D.C. All rights reserved. (*This is my favorite translation of the Psalms.*)

New American Bible Revised Edition (NABRE), Copyright © 2010, 1986 Confraternity of Christian Doctrine, Washington, D.C. All rights reserved. (*This is the current Catholic translation.*)

New Revised Standard Version Bible: Catholic Edition, Copyright © 1993 and 1989 by the Division of Christian Education of the National Council of the Churches of Christ in the U.S.A.

The New Jerusalem Bible, Copyright © 1985 by Darton, Longman & Todd, Ltd. & Doubleday, a division of Bantam Doubleday Dell Publishing Group, Inc.

The Jewish Study Bible, Copyright © 1985, 1999 by the Jewish Publication Society

Acknowlegements, continued

The Interlinear NIV Hebrew-English Old Testament, by John R. Kohlenberger III, Copyright © 1979, 1980, 1982, 1985, 1987 by the Zondervan Corporation

The NRSV-NIV Parallel New Testament in Greek and English, by Alfred Marshall, Copyright © 1990 by the Zondervan Corporation

The New Greek-English Interlinear New Testament, translators Robert K. Brown & Philip W. Comfort, Copyright © 1990 by Tyndale House Publishers

I am especially grateful for these three, and to all those who worked on the *New American Bible* Psalms of 1991.

The summary of *Lectio Divina* (on page 165) comes from many guides, all of whom have my deep gratitude, especially Rev. Paul Wachdorf of Mundelein Seminary, north of Chicago.

For more information about the Psalms of Saint Francis of Assisi see *The Geste of the Great King* by Laurent Gallant, OFM and Andre Cirino, OFM, © 2001 The Franciscan Institute, Saint Bonaventure University, New York.

These works were also very helpful:

The New Jerome Biblical Commentary, edited by Raymond E. Brown, S.S., Joseph A. Fitzmyer, S.J., and Roland E. Murphy, O.Carm., Copyright © 1990, 1968 by Prentice-Hall, Inc.

The following volumes from the **Anchor Bible**:

Psalms I (1-50); Psalms II (51-100); Psalms III (101-150), The Anchor Bible, Volumes 16, 17, and 17A, by Mitchell Dahood, S.J., Copyright © 1965,1966, © 1968, © 1970, Doubleday

The Wisdom of Solomon; The Anchor Bible, Vol. 43, by David Winston, Copyright © 1979, Doubleday & Company, Inc.

Daniel, Esher and Jeremiah, the Additions; The Anchor Bible, Vol.44, by Carey A. Moore, Copyright © 1977, Doubleday & Company, Inc.

And a stack of dictionaries.

Books by Stephen Joseph Wolf

PRAYER BOOKS

Rainbow Prayer
Rainbow Psalms in 30 Days
Dawn & Dusk Rainbow
  for Ordinary Time
Dawn & Dusk Rainbow Prayer
  (Advent, Christmas, Lent,
  Easter, & Ordinary Time)
A Jesus Breviary
31 Days of God's Love-Call
31 Days of Jesus Sayings
Pocket Retreat

FAITH SHARING ETC BOOKS

Pondering Our Faith
Tree of Life
Forty Penances for Spiritual Exercise
The Passion in the Great Story of Jesus
The Resurrection in the...Story of Jesus
God's Ones: Living in the Lord
Being Spouses
God's Money
Twelve-Step Spirituality for Christians
Anger the Jesus Way
Planning My Own Funeral?

POETRY — *Seeking Holy Honesty*

ESSAY — *Gay Respect in the Good News*

UKULELE SONGBOOKS — *Three-Finger Chord Ukulele Hymns*
Three-Finger Chord Ukulele Old-Timey Songs

Stephen Joseph Wolf is retired, a former parish priest (22 lents & holy weeks), spiritual director and retreat leader, and former certified public accountant (14 tax seasons), and before that worked as a landscaper, desk clerk, laundry worker, janitor, paper boy, and student, growing up the second of eight sons of a parish secretary and Nashville's best television repairman. He continues to write for faith-sharing groups and retreats, paint folk art icons, sing baritone for the LGBTQ+ chorus *Nashville in Harmony*, play the ukulele with *Music for Seniors* and others, volunteer as bookkeeper for two non-profits, serve on the board of *PFLAG Nashville*, and lives in Nashville with his husband Billy.   **www.idjc.org**

PSALMS

Psalm	Page	Psalm	Page	Psalm	Page
19	104	86	108	119	68
23	94	90	73	121	98
34	90	91	110	122	35
40	66	92	88	126	26
42	36	93	47	127	55
43	96	100	92	128	76
46	117	104a	78	131	106
51	113	104b	81	133	86
63	52	113	43	139	100
65	115	115	62	146	44
67	57	117	25	147a	120
80	83	118	30	147b	53
84	102	119	70	148	41

CANTICLES

Isaiah 2	58
Isaiah 55	72
Wisdom 9	38
Daniel 3:52-57	64
Daniel 3:57-90	48
Luke 1:46-55	173
Luke 1:68-79	172
Luke 2:29-32	174
Ephesians 1	27
Philippians 2	59
Revelation 4-5	33
Revelation 15	50

INDEX

READINGS

Genesis 1:27-31	63
Deuteronomy 10:12-13	67
Song of Songs 8:7	55
Wisdom 1:13-15	87
Wisdom 7:13-14	46
Jeremiah 6:16a	89
Jeremiah 31:31-33	71
Ezekiel 36:24-26	99
Micah 6:8	91
Matthew 6:25-26,31-33	65
Matthew 8:1-3	97
Matthew 8:23-27	121
Matthew 11:28-30	75
Mark 3:1-5	101
Mark 6:1-3a	83
Mark 16:5-6	93
Luke 6:17-19	112
Luke 17:20-21	114
John 14:1-7	116
Romans 8:14-17	109
Romans 8:22-27	105
Romans 8:35,37-39	34
Romans 12:1-2	40
1 Corinthians 12:24b-26	69
1 Corinthians 13:4-9,13	77
1 Corinthians 15:3-8	95
2 Corinthians 12:14b	103
Galatians 4:4-5	61
Ephesians 2:8-10	86
Ephesians 2:11-22	28
Ephesians 3:16-22	118
Philippians 3:7-9a	51
Colossians 1:12-20	107
1 John 3:17-18	73
1 John 4:9-11	80

PSALMS of FRANCIS of ASSISI

1st *Gethsemane*	137
2nd *The Sanhedrin*	139
3rd *Morning Sun*	130, 133, 140, 152
4th *Pontius Pilate*	142
5th *The Cross*	144
6th *Death on the Cross*	146
7th *Acclamation of the Christ*	123, 136, 150
8th *Echos of Struggle & Victory*	135, 151
9th *The New Song*	148
10th *Shout of Joy*	126
11th *Cry of Hope*	127
12th *Prayer of a Child*	128
13th *Time of Expectaion*	124
14th *Vision of Fulfillment*	124
15th *Origin and Birth of Christ*	131
Closing Praises	175

IMAGES by STEPHEN JOSEPH WOLF

Alleluia	149
Anger the Jesus Way	77
Baptism of the Lord	24
Crucifixion	143
Footwasher Royal	80
Hildegard Mandala	112
Holy Family in Egypt	119
Light of Christ	56
Mother of Tenderness	60
Nativity	122
Unity in Trinity	69

MORNING

CANTICLE of ZECHARIAH (The Benedictus)
LUKE 1:68-79

+ Blessed be the Lord the God of Israel
who chose a people to visit with redemption,
and raised salvation in the house of David,
saving strength from God's own servant,

speaking from the age of the prophets
through the mouth of the holy prophet:
Salvation out of enmity,
even out of those who hate us,

to show our ancestors how mercy works, -
and to remember the holy promise of the Lord,
the covenant made for our ancestor Abraham,
calming our fear and making us free
to serve with holy justice before God all our days.

And you also child -
will be called a prophet of the Most High
for you will go before the Lord to prepare his way
and give to people a knowledge of salvation
known in accepting forgiveness of their sins.

From the tender mercy of our God,
the sun rising from the height will visit with light
for those who sit in the dark or shadow of death
and to guide our feet into the way of peace.

Glory...   •

EVENING

CANTICLE of MARY (The Magnificat)
LUKE 1:46-55

+ My soul is stretched full with praise of the Lord,
and my spirit, beyond joy in God, my Savior,
who chose to lay eyes on this humble servant.

Behold, now and forward,
each and every age will call me blessed,
for the Mighty One did great things to me.

Holy is the name and the mercy
to generations and generations,
the ones fearing the One,

Who scattered the haughty of mind and heart,
pulled the powerful off their high place,
and lifted with dignity the humble in need.

The hungering are filled with good things,
the rich are sent away empty,
and servant Israel is given relief

with a memory of mercy to remember,
the promise spoken to our ancestors,
to Abraham and his descendants forever.

Glory…

●

NIGHT

Psalm 91 (see page 110) is often used for night prayer.

RESPONSORY   Ps 31:6

Into your hands, Lord, I commend my spirit;
you have redeemed us, Lord, God of truth.

CANTICLE of SIMEON
LUKE 2:29-32

Antiphon *Protect us Lord as we stay awake,*
watch over us as we sleep
that awake we may keep watch with Christ
and asleep rest in his peace.

or Lord, save/ us!
Save/ us while\ we are a-wake\,
pro-tect us while we are a-sleep,
that we may keep our watch/ with Christ/,
and when we sleep\, rest/ in his\ peace.

+ Now, **Master**, you set free your servant
according to your word in peace;

my eyes have seen the salvation,
which you have prepared
before the face of all the peoples,

a light for revelation to the nations
and glory for your people, Israel.

Glory...   Antiphon

Closing Praises

Saint Francis Psalm of Praise for All Hours
Rev 4:8, 4:11, 5:12, 19:5; Dan 3:57; Ps 69:35a,

Holy, **holy**, **holy** is the Lord God Almighty,
who was, who is, and who is to come;

R: ***Praise the Lord to forever.***

Worthy are you, our Lord and our God,
to receive the glory and honor and power;   R:

Worthy is the Lamb who was given to receive
the power and riches and wisdom and blessing;   R:

Bless the Abba and the Son and the Holy Spirit;   R:

Bless the Lord, all you works of the Lord;   R:

All you servants of the Lord, praise our God,
you small and you great, who revere God in awe;   R:

Let heaven and earth give praise;   R:

Every creature in heaven and on earth and under
the earth with the seas and all moving in them;   R:

Glory...

PRAYER of FRANCIS of ASSISI

**Almighty, most holy, you who alone are
totally good, may we give back to you all praise,
all glory, all grace, all honor, all blessing,
and all good. So be it. So be it. Amen.**

+

www.ingramcontent.com/pod-product-compliance
Lightning Source LLC
Chambersburg PA
CBHW072013110526
44592CB00012B/1293